The Joy of Books

Confessions of a Lifelong Reader

Eric Burns

Prometheus Books

59 John Glenn Drive
Amherst, NewYork 14228-2197

Published 1995 by Prometheus Books

99 98 97 96 95   5 4 3 2 1

Illustrations in this volume are taken from David Allen Williams, *A Celebration of Humanism and Freethought* (Amherst, N.Y.: Prometheus Books, 1995). Cover photograph courtesy of Levenger-Tools for Serious Readers: (800) 544–0880.

Library of Congress Cataloging-in-Publication Data

Burns, Eric.
    The joy of books : confessions of a lifelong reader / Eric Burns.
        p. cm.
    ISBN 1-57392-004-5 (alk. paper)
      1. Books and reading—United States. 2. Burns, Eric—Books and reading.
I. Title.
Z1103.2.B87   1995
028'.9—dc20   95-21306
                                                 CIP

Printed in the United States of America on acid-free paper.

To
Dianne Claire Wildman
patron

You spend too much time reading, Spenser.
You know more stuff that don't make you money
than anybody I know.

—Robert B. Parker
Mortal Stakes

Contents

INTRODUCTION: PAST   11

PART ONE: DISTANT PAST   23

The 700,000 Wonders of the Ancient World   25

The Sound of a Silent Bell   47

PART TWO: PRESENT   99

Deciding What to Believe   101

A Place of One's Own   131

EPILOGUE: FUTURE   159

THE JOY OF BOOKS LIST   181

INTRODUCTION

PAST

Illustration from an article about Angelica Kauffmann, in John Forbes-Robertson, *The Great Painters of Christendom* (New York: Cassell & Co., 1877), p. 264.

*T*he first important book in my life was *Peter Pan* by Sir James M. Barrie, and I took it to extremes. Sat on an old mattress in the basement, leaned against the wall, felt cool beads of moisture ooze out of the cinder blocks and onto my back. Propped up my knees, wedged the book into my lap. Opened cover, flipped pages, focused eyes—and then, as if cleared by the control tower and cradled by tailwinds, I lifted off, gaining altitude rapidly, and in a matter of seconds soared out of sight of all who were earthbound. The illustration opposite page 47 of my childhood edition shows five figures winging through the night sky from London to Neverland, but all internal indices registered a sixth. Peter, Tinker Bell, Wendy, Michael, John, and me. See? I'm the one circling Big Ben, behind the church spire, under the cloud shaped like an elephant's head. Barrie wrote about "them," but it was one of those literary devices I would learn about in high school. What he meant was "us."

> Sometimes it was dark and sometimes light, and now they were very cold and again too warm. Did they really feel hungry at times, or were they merely pretending, because Peter had such a jolly new way of feeding them? His way was to pursue birds who had food in in their mouths suitable for humans and snatch

it from them; then the birds would follow and snatch it back; and they would all go chasing each other gaily for miles, parting at last with mutual expressions of good will.

I did not swap food with the birds, did not feel the breeze flutter my clothes or look down to see turn-of-the-century London reduced to the size of a model train town. But my eyes were on the second star to the right as surely as Peter's and Tink's were, and I was bound for new and faraway realms no less than the Darling kids. In the book, they got there. On the mattress in the basement on long-ago summer afternoons, so did I.

I am half a century old now, and have to hold the page closer to my eyes than I used to. I do not read books if the type is too small, do not sit in chairs that are ergonomically unsound, and do not use lamps that are too dim or glaring. Even so, I often emerge from a long evening's read a bit battered: some aches here, a tightness there, needing to stretch like a cat too long curled on the hearth. My grip on detail has loosened, and my concentration is subject to occasional drift.

But I remember the story of *Peter Pan* as if I had read myself to sleep with it yesterday: Peter's exuberance, Tink's willfulness, the teeth-grating aura of menace projected by Captain Hook—so real to me are all these traits that they might be the descriptions of neighbors. I can still see the pirates' ship, "a rakish-looking craft foul to the hull, every beam in her detestable like ground strewn with feathers. She was the cannibal of the seas. . . ." I can still hear the whooping of the lost boys and the cackling of the sycophantic Smee and the ticking of the clock in the crocodile's stomach, counting down the minutes of Hook's cold and bitter existence. Such grand adventures we had back then—the fictional characters from Neverland and the real boy from a small steel town in west-

14

ern Pennsylvania. The book weaved a spell so perfectly shaped to the contours of my psyche that, like Peter himself, it has outlasted the years, Sir James M. Barrie's inventions become memories of my very own.

When I was young, and feeling the stress of an argument with parents or a snubbing by friends or a chocolate bar gone soft and sloppy in my pocket, I would turn to a section of my favorite book the way grownups turned to their most meaningful lines from the Bible. I did not think of Barrie's prose as holy, rather as rippling; it caught the light for me, reflected it, made so shimmery a surface that I took for granted the depths beneath, even if I was too callow back then to comprehend them.

Peter Pan, chapter 8, verse 1:

> If you shut your eyes and are a lucky one, you may see at times a shape-less pool of lovely pale colours suspended in the darkness; then, if you squeeze your eyes tighter, the pool begins to take shape, and the colours become so vivid that with another squeeze they must go on fire. But just before they go on fire you see the lagoon. This is the nearest you ever get to it on the mainland, just one heavenly moment; if there could be two moments you might see the surf and hear the mermaids singing.

I must have read about the mermaids a dozen times, two dozen, and dipped into other parts of the book almost as much. The chapter on the Never Bird was a favorite, as were the rollicking descriptions of the final shipboard battle. I got so familiar with the mechanics of measuring oneself for a hollow tree that I might have been slipping into a trunk myself, and I knew the song the pirates sang in their hiding places better than I knew "Happy Birthday."

Introduction: Past

Did so close an acquaintance begin to wear on me? To the contrary; I came eventually to think of *Peter Pan* not only as a means of transportation, but as the place that was the journey's end. It was more than a land of dreamy lagoons where mermaids sang their haunting tunes just out of reach; it was thickly wooded glens, treetop houses, mysterious underground caverns that wound sinuously from one end of the island to the other—and I visited as often as I could, stayed as long as possible, found a vacation in every chapter. I objected to the book, then, no more than one objects to the topography of any other haven in his life. What familiarity bred for me was contentment.

I suppose, in my unsophisticated way, I was feeling some of what Thomas Edward Lawrence had felt during his final year at university, long before Lowell Thomas and the other eventmongers of the world ladled their bronze over him and made him into the statue known as Lawrence of Arabia. In a letter to his mother, to whom he wrote frequently, he said:

> You know, I think, the joy of getting into a strange country in a book. . . . And it is lovely too, after you have been wandering for hours in the forest with Percivale or Sagramore le desirous, to open the door, and from over the Cherwell to look at the sun glowering through the valley-mists. Why does one not like things if there are other people about? Why cannot one make one's books live except in the night, after hours of straining? . . . If you can get the right book at the right times you taste joys— not only bodily, physical, but spiritual also, which pass one out above and beyond one's miserable self, as it were through a huge air, following the light of another man's thought. And you can never be quite the old self again. You have forgotten a little bit; or rather pushed it out with a little of the inspiration of what is immortal in someone who has gone before you.

Introduction: Past

As a boy, I was not aware of how many had gone before me, nor of how rich their legacies were. I was not ignorant, merely young; I lived on a perpetual eve of discovery, which was exciting at the time and even more exciting as I look back on it from the vantage point of four decades.

But it does not just seem distant now; it seems impractical. People don't read much anymore except for escape of the most banal variety or personal guidance of the most rigidly literal. And so the romance novels and the recipe collections for dieters, the slasher tales and the manuals for more ruthless behavior in business, the autobiographies of rock stars and television hosts who have accomplished nothing of significance in their days, not even truth in labeling, that is to say, the authorship of their own life stories.

And so the video games and the computer games and the CD-ROMs and all the other technologies that try to adapt literature to their own agendas, turn it into something at once whiz-bang and inert, try to make words come alive through the wonder of applied science, as if the mind of a dedicated reader were not the most vivifying arena of all. The technologies transmit messages to people whose attention spans started shrinking when "Sesame Street" first squeezed a day's lesson into a ten-second jingle with banjo accompaniment, people who have now reached the point at which they watch music videos with a certain restlessness, wondering why the editor doesn't cut more quickly, pick up the pace a little, throw in a bit more discontinuity.

I did not grow up in a world like this. I was not so jittery. I ask myself whether a progression of events is necessarily progress, and answer without hesitation. Reading should not have to be explained; a book should not have to be defended; a bookstore should not be enticing customers with a display window full of celebrity calendars, Microsoft software, and holographic bookmarks that show the Mighty Morphin Power Rangers kicking ass and taking names.

In time, maturity overtaking me, I outgrew Sir James M. Barrie's *Peter Pan* and began to look for new worlds to inhabit. But reading had become second nature by then, and my new worlds had their own literary heroes: Bomba the Jungle Boy, Chip Hilton and his backyard athletic club, and Frank and Joe Hardy. Then I was on to biographies of presidents and assorted freedom fighters, and next to novels, like *Animal Farm* and *Of Mice and Men,* for which I was not quite prepared, despite the seeming ease of the language.

It was somewhere in my Bomba phase that the change came. I began to realize that I was no longer reading merely to find stimulation when bored or contentment when troubled or blue skies when the soot tumbling from the western Pennsylvania steel mills draped a black canopy over my entire field of vision. What was happening now was that books were raising possibilities for me, and never before had so simple a phrase seemed so ripe with meaning. Raising possibilities. Two words, seven syllables, no hyperbole. But somehow the idea struck me as wondrous, a way to increase the content of my being, expand the very definition of life. I found myself thinking of raising possibilities as I imagined farmers thought of raising wheat or corn or soybeans. You planted a seed, and before long something that had never existed assumed a place in the world. It took root, grew, reached the stage of full flower. And it was not an isolated event; it could happen before every sunset, after every dawn, season after season after season. Yet there was magic in the process, a series of everyday miracles, and everything was different, however subtly, because of it. "You can never be quite the old self again," T. E. Lawrence had said, and the reason was not that you had lost, but gained. New selves now

18

existed within you. You could see more clearly, hear more acutely, understand more profoundly.

Possibilities had been raised.

Of course, I knew that books were not alone in this regard. Television, the new medium, could raise possibilities too, but as entertaining as they sometimes were, they hardly seemed exhilarating. Did I want to imagine myself a bellboy like Buddy Hackett's Stanley or a cheapskate like Jack Benny or a drag queen like Uncle Miltie? Too common, too silly. Did I want to pretend I lived in the coldwater flat of "The Honeymooners" or two-stepped through the ballroom of broken dreams from "Marty"? Not a chance. I already knew places like that in my town, walked by them on the way to school. Did I want my make-believe friends to be Fred and Ethel Mertz? For what possible reason? People just like the Mertzes, only not so crusty, lived across the street in real life; I played with their kids, hit baseballs into their pathetic patch of gardenias, and soaped their windows on Halloween. The possibilities that television raised, in other words, were insufficiently ennobling; for the most part, they were no more than the possibilities of the quotidian layered over with shtick.

Or with ersatz suspense. Richard Boone as Paladin, James Arness as Marshall Dillon, Jack Webb as Sgt. Friday—these were the medium's men of adventure, but they left me as cold as the comedians did. It might have been my lack of control: Paladin and Dillon and Friday decided for themselves when they would appear in my home; I had no say in the matter, and was not always in the mood for derring-do at the appointed hour. Or it might have been the predictable nature of their exploits, the lack of genuine peril I sensed, all of the shows pausing for commercials at the same time, ending in a precise thirty minutes, and starting anew at the same hour next week. The result, of course, was that the heroes always emerged from their missions rosy-cheeked and none the worse for wear. It was not easy to give my heart to those so coddled by fate.

And it was impossible to give my heart to this person named Mary Martin who showed up on the screen one night in green tights and a feathered cloche, with a toy sword in her belt and a smile on her face that made her look like a bottom-of-the-line Barbie doll—this Mary Martin person, pretending to be my cherished Pan! I bolted up in horror. This Mary Martin strutted, she crowed, she tossed back her head and put her fists on her hips. I gritted my teeth. She tried to get tough with Hook, but could only bluster; she tried to show a sensitive side when the young Darlings wanted to go home from Neverland, but all she managed was sappiness. I balled my fingers into fists, twitched them; so obviously was this Mary Martin acting, so obviously was she too old, so obviously was she *the wrong sex!* And when she flew around the children's bedroom, I could see the wires secured to her ribcage and hooked up to a mechanical device of some sort offstage. I checked back with Barrie's book. Not a single mention of wires. Just as I suspected.

And Tiger Lily was this stuck-up little Hollywood high school girl and the lost boys a pack of brats and Neverland about as enchanting as a flat from the local community theatre. What was television thinking? I could not be so selfish as to deny the new medium the right to make a public spectacle of my private vision, but neither did I have to forgive it for so brutal a dismembering of what I held precious. I am not one to bear grudges, but to this day my temples throb and my incisors grind when I think of the middle-aged woman who dared masquerade as the world's only unaging boy.

A drag *king*?

Movies also raised possibilities, but I never felt able to manage them. The screen was too large and it overwhelmed me; the actors were too famous and I could never believe in the characters they claimed to play. Movies were like the major tourist attractions to me: the Washington Monument, the Empire State Building, the Golden Gate Bridge—imposing, ornate, the obvious works of gifted individuals and highly developed engineering, but too remote to elicit a response other than awe. I could lose myself in the cocoon of a darkened theater for a few hours on a Saturday afternoon, could go home and pretend to be Tony Curtis in *The Black Shield of Falworth* for a few more, but then I started to feel self-conscious. Why Tony Curtis? What was so special, so relevant to my own life and times, about a medieval knight with a Brooklyn accent? "Hark, youse guys. Yonda lies da castle of my fodda." Whose fantasy was this anyhow, mine or some Hollywood mogul's?

Movies were more than half a century old when I was growing up, but I could not help seeing them as even more of a novelty than television, each scene a trick, a gimmick—with a fancy camera angle or an ingeniously choreographed stunt or a cartoon-like special effect that would allow a dinosaur to raze a skyscraper with a flick of its tail. Sometimes I laughed, sometimes I shivered with apprehension; unlike other kids, though, I could never make of movies a vehicle for flight.

But a book, a book: possibilities sprouted like vegetation in the wild, possibilities that were tantalizing and extraordinary, yet at the same time as easy for me to govern as a younger playmate. I could read any book I chose, in any place, at any time. I could open the book, close it, shift the angle, move it to another spot, establish complete sovereignty; it was right there in my hand, the sensation tactile as well as fanciful. I could speed up, slow down, stop altogether to consider the author's nuances; after all, "to read without reflecting," Edmund Burke said two centuries ago, "is like eating without digesting."

Introduction: Past

And with a book I could strike the perfect balance between mastery and drift. The author laid out the itinerary, telling me who the characters were and what they said and did, insisting on the wheres and whys and hows. But what the author could not do was visualize his tale for me, brand it into my consciousness. The ultimate power in reading, that of determining what will be perceived and in what manner, what will be retained and acted upon, what will be ignored—this power belonged to me. "The best of novels," Robertson Davies wrote, about the time I was entering high school and starting on O. Henry and Dickens, "are only scenarios to be completed by the reader's own experience."

And who was this reader before whom even the most accomplished of writers so graciously bowed, allowing a collaborator in the glories of artistic process? *I* was. *Me,* a nine-year-old kid who wanted to be a fireman when he grew up and then a ten-year-old who wanted to play shortstop for the Pirates and then an eleven-year-old who dreamed of parachuting behind enemy lines to win the war single-handed—a boy, I was, only a boy, but already I held a position of respect in the community of books. The passivity of the moviegoer or the blind docility of the television addict were not for me. I was a completer of literary scenarios! I might not have been the equal of my favorite authors, but I was without question an ally, someone upon whom they depended for the ultimate success of their ventures. No wonder people wrote their names in the books they bought. It was not to prove ownership; it was to take the credit they were rightfully due, share the billing with the man or woman on the title page.

But the relationship between reader and writer has evolved over the eons. In the beginning, whenever *that* was, there were few signs of closeness or shared responsibility. Writers scrawled, readers deciphered. Writers proclaimed, readers consented. In fact, it is stretching a point to think in terms of a relationship at all.

PART ONE

DISTANT PAST

Illustration from John Forbes-Robertson, *The Great Painters of Christendom* (New York: Cassell & Co., 1877), p. 32.

The 700,000 Wonders
of the Ancient World

*A*ll that can be said with certainty about the world's first writer is that he preceded the world's first formal written language. He may have been a potter who worked into an urn or vase a design that would identify the piece's eventual owner. He may have been a hunter who made crude drawings on the walls of a cave to report the day's kill. He may have been a shipper of goods, his scratches on clay tokens serving as bills of lading. Or perhaps he was a man in charge of a granary, whose markings on a stone or block of wood registered the name of the individual who had brought in his crop, as well as the amount deposited.

Whoever he was, he was not a writer as we understand the term today. He did not do second drafts, did not bemoan an uncomprehending public, did not dream of an advance on royalties large enough to buy a franchise in the National Hockey League. He was a kind of accountant. He did not create.

The world's first reader, then, was a person who accepted the notion of private property. Nothing else was required of him, nothing else given. No more could he have comprehended the tapestries that Sir James M. Barrie and others would one day weave of language than he could have comprehended thunder without angry gods. He did not read for escape, did not experience exalted feelings, was not inspired to contemplate the true nature of reality. Such responses would have to await a point in the future when the elaboration of religious beliefs prepared the human spirit for a new expansiveness—accustoming it to prodigies, releasing the powers of imagination, and encouraging an appreciation of the complexities of art in the writer as well as the reader. Art and religion are similar, says John H. Randall, Jr., a biographer of Aristotle, in that both overcome the "difficulties of matter."

Equally utilitarian was the development of books. The earliest were produced in Babylonia and Assyria more than three thousand years before Christ, with the first perhaps being a Chaldean version of the great flood, later appropriated and revised by those who wrote the Bible. Other ancient volumes collected Sumerian poems, including one in which a woman implores her newlywed husband to put his hand on her "goodly place." "Let me caress you," she goes on. "My precious caress is more savory than honey."

But the majority of books from civilization's nascent days consisted of legal documents, noting that this man sold so many animals, this one bought so many pelts, this one had in his possession the items enumerated thereafter. These were ledgers, not stories, and it was important that they be kept accurately. Says another Sumerian tome from this approximate period, "You can have a Lord, you can have a King, but the man to fear is the tax collector."

The information was set down on pages that had started out in life as handfuls of clay, gathered at riverbanks and formed into tablets. While still moist, the tablets were poked with sticks and pushed with fingertips, the primitive equivalent of printing. Then they were placed on beds of grass and left to dry in the sun, sometimes overnight, sometimes for several days, the heat making the language indelible. Finally, the tablets were bound together with straps of leather or reed, and the result, loosely speaking, was a book—baked, not published.

But clay was not always available and the sun did not always shine. In a variety of other places, people used sections of animal hide as a writing material. Thin sheets of copper served for a time in Burma, and the shoulder bones of goats, polished to a smooth gloss, in Tibet. The medium of choice in India was palm leaves, and until the second century A.D., the Chinese spelled out their transactions on pieces of bamboo and scraps of waste silk. Then they invented paper, although of a roughhewn kind, pounding hemp fibers into slabs so coarse that the individual sheets looked like welcome mats trod upon too many times.

Before long the Egyptians came up with their own version of paper, and it was a notable improvement over not only the Chinese prototype, but the fragments of limestone and broken shards of pottery upon which the Egyptians themselves had previously written. The paper was made from a reed called *Cyperus papyrus,* which grew wild along the Nile and on the shores of the Mediterranean. Once as common as scrubgrass in that part of the world, papyrus has long since become endangered vegetation. The English word "paper" derives from it; other than that, the reed has made little impression on the modern world.

Here is what the Egyptians did. They uprooted the papyrus and peeled away the bark. They sliced the stem into strips about nine inches long and pasted several of them into a sheet, with the uneven spots, where the strips overlapped, smoothed out as much as possible. They fastened the sheets together with paste, one sheet to the next, and then to the next and the next and the next, creating a single, sprawling page that sometimes reached lengths of 150 feet. Finally they attached a wooden roller to the top of the manuscript and another to the bottom, so that the final product, unopened, looked like a couple of war clubs with some wrapping paper around them. This kind of book was known as a volumen. In *The Discoverers,* Daniel Boorstin explains the difficulties of dealing with it: "The reader had to unroll the manuscript as he went along and then had to reroll the book before it could be used again, much as a motion-picture film has to be rewound after each showing. . . . No wonder that the grammarian Callimachus (305–240 B.C.), head librarian at Alexandria, said, 'A big book is a big nuisance.' "

The constant rolling and unrolling, especially when done with hands that were dirty and sweating, wore the papyrus thin and then rubbed holes through it. In time, a section of manuscript got to look as tattered as an undershirt in the final stages of a long career. Further, the inks of the time were not permanent, so the more the book was opened and closed, the more the words flaked away, until finally a person had to guess at them from the remaining context rather than actually take them in with his eyes. It was like a parlor game: fill in the blanks, predict the predicate. And since there was no way for a scroll to be paginated, it was a painstaking process for the reader to return to a certain passage, verify a certain fact. How would he remember? Would he say to himself: I think that quote was about fifty flicks of the wrist back? Maybe sixty? If I unroll for as long as it takes two clouds to pass across the midnight moon, I ought to be there?

For this reason, among others, histories of long ago are notoriously whimsical; all but the most persevering of chroniclers would rely on memory, or invent an occurrence or two, rather than search through the voluminous coils of volumens to ensure accuracy.

In centuries following, they got less voluminous. After Callimachus, and perhaps in part due to his protests, volumens with as few as 750 lines began to appear; even the longest seldom amounted to more than two hundred pages or so in modern format. But at times this proved an even bigger nuisance. The short story had not yet been invented; the epic poem flourished. *The Iliad* and *The Odyssey* each ran to thirty-six rolls, enough to prove a burden not just to the person who intended to read them, but to his family and friends and slaves, without whose contributory armloads he would not have been able to lug home more than the first few chapters. Transporting a single book at civilization's dawn could be like transporting a small library today. No wonder there were so few readers; literacy demanded too much brawn!

In what we know as its present form, the book first appeared in Rome about A.D. 300. Its pages were the specially treated skins of lamb or calf or kid called vellum, sections of which had been folded into small parcels, or gatherings. The gatherings were then sewn together to make the book, known as a codex, which, as Boorstin points out, had a variety of advantages over the volumen. It "was handy to use, more durable, more copious in content, and more compact to store." Other historians, in conversations with me, have praised the codex in grander terms. "A great boon to learning," believes one. "Perhaps mankind's first large step forward intellectually," opines another. "An unmistakable sign of progress," holds a third, "of which there had, up to that point in the development of the species, been few."

Romans of an earlier time would not have agreed. Neither would their Greek counterparts. They thought the volumen was a threat to society because it shackled words to the page; in the codex, they might have seen the northern hordes exploding through the gates.

In the beginning was the gesture, one person communicating with another by pointing to an object or drawing a picture in the air. Arms out, hands up, a finger or two extended and wiggling a little—the more important the topic, the more exaggerated the wiggle. In this way were statements made, questions raised, exclamations uttered. In this way did the limbs declaim.

Then came the grunt, the rough draft of human speech, the sound our forebears made in inadvertent accompaniment to the gesture, or in conscious imitation of what they happened to hear in nature. Or, as Jean Jacques Rousseau seemed to think, "to implore assistance in case of danger, or relief in case of suffering." Ooof, aaah, grrr. Whooo, hmmm, ugh. Humble beginnings, a long way to Mario Cuomo, not nearly so far to Howard Stern.

But over the centuries the grunt developed into something more complex and varied, the process aided by early man's realization that spoken words were superior to gestures because they could be employed in the dark, and even in the light left the hands free to perform other tasks. Also aiding the process, as anthropologist Helen Fisher explains, was our ancestors' decision to raise up on their hind legs and walk erect, which caused the larynx to sink into the throat, so that the air emitted between the vocal chords had farther to travel to the mouth. This means, says Fisher, that "new sophisticated sounds could be uttered." The grunt became a word or two, then a series of words, then a modest vocabulary.

The first words were almost surely nouns, the identification of objects and various natural processes. Verbs followed in due course, describing different kinds of deeds, actions taken by or upon the nouns. It all had a kind of geological inevitability to it, the poet Walt Whitman would one day conclude, "with its ceaseless evolution, its fossils, and its numberless submerged layers and hidden strata, the infinite go-before of the present."

For thousands of years, the words that people spoke were the only ones that existed; from philosopher to pupil, parent to child, mate to mate, all that was known and believed and feared and imagined was related aloud. There was a path from mouth to ear;

civilization followed it. No one was peeling away papyrus bark yet, or polishing goat bones; there was no such noun as "book," no such verb as read.

Today we refer to the exclusivity of spoken language as the oral tradition, and it was not as provincial as it sounds. "The range and fecundity of the traditional oral language," says the *Oxford History of the Classical World,* "should not be underestimated." Nor was it, by those who have thought on the matter. The Greek historian Thucydides implies that fellow historian Herodotus could attribute his "powers of intelligent analysis and anticipatory foresight" directly to his mastery of the spoken word. Contemporary historian Michael Grant suggests the same for the "outstanding intellect" of the polymath Protagoras, the "encyclopaedic competence" of the tyrant Hippias, and the "rhythmical, flowery, exciting prose-style" of the philosopher Gorgias. As a young man, Homer learned to compose poetry by listening to the recitations of older bards, copying their styles and in many cases their exact phrases. Nothing was written. No one knew how. No one felt a need.

The foundation of the oral tradition was Memory, which the rhetorician Cicero went so far as to capitalize and to anoint one of the five principal parts of rhetoric. One of Cicero's successors, Quintilian, described the importance of the so-called architectural system of memorization. It has been summarized as follows:

> Think of a large building ... and walk through its numerous rooms remembering all the ornaments and furnishings in your imagination. Then give each idea to be remembered as an image, and as you go through the building again deposit each image in this order in your imagination. For example, if you mentally deposit a spear in the living room, an anchor in the dining room, you will later recall that you are to speak first of the war, then of the navy, etc. This system still works.

Part One: Distant Past

The importance of memory to a world without written language cannot be overstated. Compare it to the importance of fire to a world without industrial processes, or of the wheel to a world without means of conveyance save what the human ankle appends to the leg. In the age before history, a person's mind was volumen and codex, VCR and warehouse, floppy disc and Post-It pad. It was library, warehouse, and vault. The more skilled an individual was in the practice of memory's arts, the more valuable the services he could perform for his community; he could ground it in the present, link it to the past, make it believe in a future. Some scholars wonder whether Homer was deliberately blinded by the elders of his tribe so that he would not be tempted to stray. Primitive times, primitive displays of regard.

And so the challenge presented by the written word cannot be overstated, either. Few people at the time accepted the notion that the visible symbols of the page came in peace, that they meant to supplement the oral tradition, aid in the retention and enrichment of learning, ease the constant struggles of memory. More common was the fear that written language would foster laziness, making the muscles of the mind flabby by requiring less of them. According to this view, the result, over time, would be a loss of society's values, customs, and lore: a loss, in other words, of society itself. What cannot be remembered cannot be repeated; what cannot be repeated can no longer exist. The way would be prepared, literally, for the northern hordes.

Few of the ancients dreaded the decline of memory as much as Socrates, father of methodical reasoning and mother hen of the spoken word. In the *Phaedrus,* he warns that written language is almost perversely accessible, communication of easy virtue, and as such, brings on idleness and languor, leading people to be spectators of debate rather than participants, couch potatoes long before the couch. Socrates was also apprehensive about what we would today refer to as targeting the audience. "Once a word is written," Socrates has been quoted as saying, "it goes rolling all about, comes indifferently among those who understand it . . . and is unaware to whom it should address itself and to whom it should not do so."

The master's best-known pupil, Plato, did not feel so strongly. Nonetheless, as a child of the oral tradition, he was anxious about the advance of the written word, dubious that its intent was benign. In one of his orations, he seems to dismiss writing as a fad, maintaining that "no man of intelligence will venture to express his philosophical views in language, especially language that is unchangeable, which is true of that which is set down in written characters." In other words, Plato was critical of what later generations would regard as a principal virtue of writing: its permanence. To Plato it seemed too confining, uncompromising. What if a person wanted to change his mind, expand on a point, shift the emphasis? What if, growing wiser with the years, he sought to amend the errors of youth? The printed page would not allow it; the writer would forever be chained to the mistakes of his past.

Even as late as the eighteenth century, a friend of Benjamin Franklin named Michael Welfare was expressing the same trepidation. He did not want the theology of his sect, the Dunkers, to be "bound" by paper, nor did he want Dunkers of the future to believe that "what we their elders and founder had done" was "something sacred, never to be departed from." The spoken word is a breeze, the written word an engraving upon stone; as by far the more flexible, the former seemed better suited to the vicissitudes of human nature.

But by the time Plato confessed his doubts, they were obsolete. The book had already become an established forum, and Plato, however reluctantly, was so skilled a convert that his objections smacked of hypocrisy. As Neil Postman reminds us in *Teach-*

ing as a Conserving Activity, it was "Plato who wrote the arguments against writing that we attribute to Socrates."

Yet reports of the oral tradition's death were exaggerated. Volumens and codices were read aloud so often that they might have been cue cards rather than books. Hearing the words made them real for people who lived in an age of superstition and shadow; it made thoughts almost as tangible as the crops they grew or the animals they hunted, and therefore as easy to exchange with others.

But the means by which markings on a page were conveyed to the reader's brain, being silent as well as unobservable, were mysterious, untrustworthy. What proof was there that written language would arrive at the brain as planned? How would it get there? What might happen to it en route? There was a path from mouth to ear, yes; but from papyrus to pate? No one had ever imagined such a thing, and that being the case, this whole writing business seemed a clandestine operation at best, turning words into sneak thieves, agents of sorcery; if nothing else, there loomed the possibility that a jealous god would intervene, insisting that matters so otherworldly in scope were best left to the immortals. Maybe the god would throw a shroud over whatever meaning the author intended. Maybe the letters and symbols would vanish at some point; what was holding them to the page? Maybe the page would erupt in flame; who was to say it couldn't? And maybe, given the high rate of illiteracy at the time, even if the words did complete their journey to the brain, they would not be understood.

If they were read aloud, though, so that the ear was enlisted in the cause, the odds of achieving comprehension would be much greater. Hearing was evidence that the senses were actively involved, providing a fallback system that guaranteed successful communication. Most people found it reassuring.

The bishop of Milan scoffed. Alvin Toffler tells us in *Power-shift* that, five centuries after Christ, St. Augustine referred to the bishop, whom he considered his mentor, as the smartest person in the world, and offered as proof the fact that the bishop could grasp the significance of an author's words without making a sound or even moving his lips. Let others practice such cautions; the bishop preferred to read to himself, eschewing the oral tradition, and almost everyone who knew him agreed it was a feat of incomparable daring.

Some, though, had misgivings. While conceding the bishop's abilities, they privately thought him addled, a loose player with fate, much as people today would think a fellow foolish who blindfolded himself and hopped along the westbound lanes of the Ventura Freeway on an eastbound pogo stick during the afternoon rush hour. We would admire the skill, but question the point.

Even a thousand years after the bishop, it was so common for books to be pronounced in full voice that hoarseness was a frequent affliction of the well-read. In fact, there was a certain cachet to it—a raspy throat equaled a cultivated mind. As for authors, they would read aloud for reasons of their own. Molière, for example, got an initial reaction to his plays by reciting them to his cook, making sure that he gasped at the coincidence, winked at the innuendo, all reactions present and in their proper places. A century later, Jane Austen tested her novels by making a formal presentation of them to friends and visitors. One imagines the scene, hearing a faint tinkle of harpsichord in the background as she does so.

A carriage pulls up to the Austen manse and the doorbell is rung. The author herself answers, smiling graciously, and shows her guests to seats in the parlor, where earlier arrivals have already begun to partake of tea and biscuits. There are comments on the weather, some inquiries about health, a general air of subdued expectancy. Then the cups and plates are removed and silence settles over the assemblage like mist over the moors. Harpsichord out. The author positions herself in the front of the room, clears her throat, and launches into the third chapter of *Mansfield Park*, the passing of old Mr. Norris, "which happened when Fanny was about fifteen, and necessarily introduced alterations and novelties."

As Miss Austen reads, her eyes flit up, work the room, monitoring the effects of her prose. Is anyone yawning, looking away, scratching an imaginary itch? Are there coughs, shiftings of torso and derriere in the chairs? How many people are leaning forward, hanging on the next words, curious about those necessary alterations and novelties? The author is like a comedian trying out new material on a weeknight at the Improv, sensitive to any nuance that will tell her whether it plays poorly or well.

For the most part, there are no signs of displeasure, which is hardly surprising given not only the quality of the author's prose but the fact that it was she who packed the house in the first place. A biographer of Miss Austen, Max Wilk, assures us that a social gathering of this sort, hosted not only by Jane Austen but by numerous other writers of the period, "was the ordinary practice."

Far less ordinary, and much more frostily received, were readings by the child Antoine de Saint-Exupéry early in the present century. "He wrote his poems mostly at night," Stacy Schiff relates in her biography, *Saint-Exupéry*,

> when he prowled the house in search of an audience. Draped in a blanket or a tablecloth, he routinely woke his brother and sisters for dramatic readings of his newly minted verse. His protesting siblings in tow, he then led the way to Madame de Saint-Exupéry's room, where he would light a lamp and energetically repeat his performance, often prevailing until 1:00

A.M. His explanation for these intrusions was simple: "When you are awakened abruptly in such a way, you have a much greater clearness of mind," he informed his mother.

Even today, even to an empty room, an author who truly cares about his work will read it audibly. He will pick up his typescript as if opening the door to a cage, and by speaking his words aloud, set them free. He will listen as they ascend from the page, bouncing off the walls of his study and back again, returning to him in what is, in terms of cadence, their natural state. The writer will concentrate fully, attuned to no other sounds and to no sights at all. "I find it necessary," John Steinbeck once said of his recitations, "for the sake of the rhythms." Putting himself into the place of readers like me, the writer will make sure there are no missed beats to distract us from his literary designs. In this way, and in no other, can he gauge the relationship between sense and sound that distinguishes superior prose from fundraising speeches by a city council candidate in Bethesda, Maryland.

The commercially successful author will hear his words through another voice as well: a mildly successful actor reading them into a tape recorder. The author gets a free copy of the cassette and listens to it at his convenience, while consumers pay for the product and tune in as they drive cars, ride buses, take trains, pedal bicycles, stroll along sidewalks, jog through parks, push lawn mowers, walk pets, shop for food, cook dinner, wash dishes, defrost refrigerators, dust living rooms, paint bathrooms, and gaze at lonely horizons from the balconies of time-share condos. This is the phenomenon known as books on tape, the oral tradition *redivivus,* the age of technology tipping its hat to the age of stone. As of 1994, there were more than fifty thousand literary titles available on cassette from some 1,400 publishers. In principle, Socrates would have been pleased. It is unlikely, though, that such specific applications as Jenny Agutter reciting Sidney Sheldon's *Memories of Midnight* would have restored his faith in the ultimate course of civilization.

So the early alarms about the demise of the spoken word have proven to be false. And far from being a death knell to effective communication, the page has been a boon, leading to greater precision, richness, and reliability than was ever possible through the oral tradition alone. The page has spread literacy, not destroyed cultures, encouraged storytelling, not rendered it obsolete. It has promoted complexity, furthered diversity, become a tradition of its own. And perhaps more important, it has stimulated, not diminished, the powers of the human mind. "The strongest memory," the Chinese like to say, "is weaker than the palest ink."

The most famous library of early days, a "cage of the Muses," was in Alexandria, Egypt, presided over for a time by the same Callimachus who so objected to the big book. But no traces of the building remain at present, and there are no reliable sketches, so it is not known how large the library was, how elegant, how exhilarating. It is not known what men thought as they luxuriated in primitive knowledge, considered its sources, imagined its implications. And it is not known what caused the library to vanish from the face of the earth. Fire? Invaders? Natural disaster? The march of the centuries?

What *is* known is that the library at Alexandria was more than just a place where books were stored; it was also a publishing house, under the aegis of which, as Will Durant relates in *The Life of Greece,* some authors

> wrote histories of various departments of literature or science, others edited definitive editions of the masterpieces, others composed commentaries on these texts for the enlightenment of

laity and posterity. . . . By the end of the third century the Museum, the Library, and their scholars had made Alexandria, in everything but philosophy, the intellectual capital of the Greek world.

But during the reign of Ptolemy III, the Alexandrian library became an institution as intrusive as it was grand. A traveler who entered the city with a manuscript among his belongings was required to check it at the gates or the port, and was given a receipt. Upon departing, he would find a copy of the book awaiting him; the original went to the library, where it was rolled up in a jar and placed on a shelf like so much preserved fruit, knowledge to be consumed at a later date. The forfeited volumen was the price of admission to one of antiquity's great lands, and so many people paid it that a thriving hotel and restaurant trade developed at the library's virtual doorstep.

But in an even greater land there were books that the third Ptolemy coveted far more than those already in his catalogue. Some had been written by the Greek playwrights: Sophocles, whose characters sought truth and understanding at the expense of all else; Euripides, the early master of psychology and social criticism; and Aeschylus, whose language was sublime and whose themes were tragic. Other books elaborated upon history and speculated upon governance and speculated even further about the gods. All in all, the books were a treasure trove of early Greek learning and creative expression, and Ptolemy's craving for them moved him first to envy, then to deceit. He sent a message to Athens that he would like to borrow the works for a time, to feast his eyes upon them and allow his scholars to educate themselves through their bounty. As a show of good faith, Ptolemy promised to make a security deposit equivalent to more than a hundred thousand dollars in today's money. The Greeks took the deal.

Part One: Distant Past

Ptolemy took the Greeks. The manuscripts were delivered to Alexandria, scrupulously copied, and the copies went back to Athens. Ptolemy kept the originals, figuring that a hundred grand was a pittance to pay for works so brilliantly composed. Perhaps it was at this time when one of Callimachus's successors as administrator of the library declared that among its 700,000 volumens was a copy of practically every scroll then known to exist, containing almost all of the world's knowledge and hearsay and superstition. It was an outrageous claim. There is no reason to doubt it.

Security at Alexandria and other libraries of the distant past was tight. Soldiers were posted inside or out or both, usually carrying weapons, and these were men used to behaving violently even when provocation was slight. Laws were stringent, leniency out of the question; books were as rare a commodity at the time as jewels, and in their own way no less valuable. Thus most libraries did not allow them to be removed from the premises, and in some cases chained their books to the walls, so that they could be perused no farther from the shelves than the length of the iron links. Those who managed to abscond with a volume anyhow might find themselves at peril from an authority higher than the temporal. "This book belongs to St. Mary of Robert's Bridge," said the inscription in a codex from a twelfth-century archive. "Whosoever shall steal it, or sell it, or in any way alienate it from this house, or mutilate it, let him be forever accursed. Amen."

Such is the degree to which knowledge was esteemed at a time when ignorance was mankind's greatest curse. Such is the extent to which enlightenment was prized in ages that have since come to be regarded as dark.

Most books of ancient vintage were produced not in libraries but in monasteries, sweatshops of the Lord, perched atop mountains or tucked into valleys, out of sight of secular life and insulated by piety as much as remoteness. Inside lived men who had no use for the world as other men had fashioned it. They pooled their property and tended to crops. They read the Scriptures and humbly beseeched the heavenly father who had inspired them. And, with steady hand and indomitable mien, they created new manuscripts or made copies of existing ones, the work of such quantity that few breaks in the day were possible, and of such an exacting nature that a sneeze could ruin an entire week's output.

Yet few were the scribes who rebelled, fewer still those who broke their vows of silence long enough to complain. Instead, they rolled up the sleeves of their hair shirts, bent over their desks, and went about the business of preserving the larger part of western literature. They wrote down myth and conjecture, miracle and daily occurrence, virtually everything that was not outright heresy, and sometimes even that—the better to construct a disavowal. Almost all of what remains of early Latin poetry and prose has been handed down to us, literally, by the monks of ancient Europe. No matter that little of the stuff is known today and even less of it read; the manuscripts turned out in monasteries were the great archaeological digs of early intellect, the sources from which historians have learned the vast majority of what they know about medieval thought and deed. "To remain ignorant of things that happened before you were born," Cicero wrote more than two thousand years ago, "is to remain a child." If that is so, the modern world owes much of its maturity to the men who toiled in the holy sweatshops of centuries long past.

Not that the monks had future generations in mind. Their primary concern was heavenly reward, the carrot at the end of mortality's stick. They believed that by copying manuscripts they served their maker as diligently as if they prayed or fasted or flagellated themselves with metal-tipped lashes, especially if the volumes they crafted were religious in nature, as almost all of them were. "It is a noble work to write out holy books," said an English monk of the eighth century, quoted by Daniel Boorstin, "nor shall the scribe fail of his due reward. Writing books is better than planting vines, for he who plants a vine serves his belly, but he who writes a book serves his soul."

Some monasteries, going further, offered employee incentive programs, decreeing that for each line of manuscript a monk copied, he would have one of his sins forgiven by the powers above. Not a bad deal. A single edition of the Bible contained tens of thousands of lines; by the time he finished transcribing them, even a highwayman could be pure of heart.

To manufacture their goods with maximum efficiency, the monks often divided themselves into four groups. The first prepared the writing surface, which was either vellum or parchment, the former for more stylish tomes, often to be housed in the grand cathedrals of the time. As for the latter, made of sheepskin from which the hair and stray pieces of flesh had been carefully plucked, sheets were commonly used more than once. In this case, the monks had to scrape away the old writing to make room for the new. The refurbished sheet was called a palimpsest, and might itself be scraped of its contents at some point in the future, turned into a palimpsest of the second or third generation. It was an admirable economy of material, but in the process the monks may have copied over almost as much history as they saved.

The second group did the actual writing, but those who comprised it did not consider themselves authors. Secretaries in the service of the Almighty is more like it; their God spoke to them in His various ways and the monks took down the words exactly as they understood them, careful not to interject any of their own personalities or ideas. They would not presume such a thing. Theirs was a higher calling than mere self-expression, which was as foreign a concept at the time as self-restraint is to the present era.

The writers used pens of quill or reed, and a variety of inks, black and colored, made from berries, the internal organs of cuttlefish, and almost everything else that lent itself, however crudely, to liquefaction. "One twelfth century monk," writes Catherine Oakes in her children's book, *The Middle Ages,* "described how he made red ink from copper, salt, honey and urine. The process took him four weeks! Some red inks were made from crushed insects. Sometimes real gold was even used."

Initially, the monks printed their letters an inch or so high, half an inch wide, in the style of script known as "majuscule." The object, like that of today's large print books, was to make reading possible for the visually impaired. But this was *not* an admirable economy of material; too much paper was required to house too few words. So in the eighth century, around the time of Charlemagne, scribes began to shrink their writing into "minuscule" script. Later, in accordance with the flourishes developing in architecture, the small letters got fancier, whorls and hooks and curlicues now adorning them—the writing, like the buildings, known to us as Gothic.

Minuscule is harder to read than majuscule. Minuscule with frou-frous is harder to read than minuscule that has not been gussied up. But what makes certain medieval manuscripts almost impossible for modern eyes to decipher is the absence of punctuation. An admirable economy of ink. There were few commas, periods or question marks, little in the way of spacing between words, and hardly any indenting for paragraphs. None of this became the general practice, historians tell us, until well into the fifteenth century.

The third group of monks consisted of artists, not copyists, men who decorated the manuscripts by splashing on color, highlighting important passages, making the hooks more pronounced and the curlicues curlier. Illumination, this was called, as if the pictures somehow shone a light on the otherwise drab parchment or vellum. The artists provided full and partial pages of drawing, and to other pages added borders and designs which, despite the limitations of space and material, often had a kind of grandeur to them.

At this point, the scribes joined the artists to look over a book and check for mistakes. Quality control it was, and the monks were as zealous about it as a team of Toyota engineers on an all-night caffeine jag. Breathing slowed as the pages were inspected; hearts stopped when errors were found, errors which were in some cases interpreted as a form of blasphemy, a visual sin against the manuscript's holy intent. Small slips of the pen could be corrected easily: a drip turned into a new motif of some sort, the wrong letter made right through some jimmying and jiggling. Blunders of greater scale, though, required more effort, and at one particular monastery, a generous helping of ingenuity. In *The Story of Writing*, calligrapher Donald Jackson tells of a monk who,

> having missed out a whole section of the text, had no option but to write out the missing lines in the margin at the bottom of the page, and make fun of his own mistakes by having the illuminator crate up the missing words in a decorative box, harness it with ropes and paint in a team of little men to haul the words contained in the crate to their rightful place in the text.

"More frequently," Jackson writes, "a missing word which could not be squeezed in was written in the margin in ink, and a helpful pointing finger would show the reader where to place it."

The fourth group of monks handled distribution. In addition to shipping books to churches and the odd secular library, they traded them with their fellows in other monasteries, or filed them away on their own shelves. "A monastery without a library," wrote a brother in Normandy in 1170, "is like a castle without an armory. . . . Thence it is that we bring forth the sentences of the Divine Law like sharp arrows to attack the enemy."

Many of the persons who read the manuscripts were servants of the Lord themselves, and the experience must have been overwhelming for them. More often than not, these were men who led lives of punishing hardship and denial, with solitude to keep them company, poverty to remind them of their earthly station, and only faith to sustain them, a faith that at times must have seemed so unrequited as to be a delusion. Where were the signs of the Almighty's hand? Where were there even hints, little reminders to keep the faith? In the splendors of nature, of course, but this was beauty without a soul. In the hearts of men and women, of course, but not all of them and not all the time; human beings could be capricious, undependable, even evil. At appointed hours each day, the clerics would drop to their knees, bow their heads, and beg their creator for some tiny shred of proof that they believed not idly, lived not in vain.

And then what should these poor men encounter in the midst of their barrenness but visual symbols become the word of God! It must have seemed like magic to them, like alchemy. For so long they had dreamed of the Second Coming—perhaps this was the form it had taken. Letters as messengers, words as agents most sacred, winged pages from realms celestial and everlasting. Minuscule, majuscule, majesty!

Accounts from the time tell us of virtual orgies, men of the cloth gone so greedy with their own copies of the Bible or some lesser Christian tome that they refused to lift their eyes from it, refused to stop their fingers from caressing the paper, making their devotion into a sensuous matter, even though they might be sitting on hard, backless benches, their spines compressing as if

45

locked in a vise, cold and hungry and alone. But not nearly so alone as they had been before the holy written word. All day they would stare and touch their volumes like creatures possessed; at night they lit candles, and the pages flickered in their hands like beacons sending out messages over a sea of black.

What it all meant was that the printed page became a building block of the early church no less than stones and mortar, and the men who led the prayers for others were now assured that their belief had not been misplaced after all, their lives not wasted. Their commitment to the Almighty was not merely strengthened by the appearance of written language; it was formalized, made eternal, and their appreciation for His marvelous powers was magnified a hundredfold and more.

The first reader understood private property. Those who came later understood salvation. Humanity's belief in a divine authority made reading a supernatural experience in the Middle Ages. To men and women of willing spirit, it remains one to this day.

The Sound of a Silent Bell

*B*ut not everyone thought of books as a blessing. Some people disagreed with their premises; others resented their implications; still others feared their consequences. To these individuals the written word was a foe, and they went to war against it, their goal to destroy the offending symbols on their encampments of paper and to remove all traces of the meaning with which they had been armed. Battles raged; casualties mounted; military metaphors rang with appropriateness—and not just to the monk a few pages back who compared a library to an armory. A censor, after all, is as bellicose in his way as a soldier in his; both mean to impose goals of ideology through the use of force, and neither takes kindly to attempts at compromise.

History's first censor of note may have been the Athenian lawgiver Solon, whose virtues were many. He freed slaves, established popular courts, extended the voting franchise, revised an inefficient monetary system to facilitate foreign trade, and reformed the domestic economy by cancelling agricultural debts and redistributing wealth. Solon was, as C. V. Wedgwood has written, a man "of strong character and good judgment." Under his rule, Athens took important first steps along the road to the democracy for which it is so revered today.

Yet there was within him a tyrant born of certainty, his belief in the correctness of his views an absolute, as was his conviction that those who took issue with him did so at the expense of the common weal. Solon made it a crime to speak ill of the living in public and of the dead anywhere. He also outlawed the writing and delivery of lengthy addresses at funerals, and, in Will Durant's words, "condemned pompous ceremonies" of all sorts. In some cases, the punishment was slight, a fine or a form of public humiliation; in others, the miscreant lost his citizenship. A government has a right to regulate the words that its citizens read and write and speak: that seemed the Solonian principle, the response of one learned man to the rapid development of language and the communicative arts. It was a principle that would be adopted by countless other rulers in ages to come.

A century and a half later, in fact, the principle would prove to be the undoing of one of Greece's leading citizens. As the founder of European grammar and philology, as well as a leading figure in the formulation of rules for modern debate, Protagoras was among the more open-minded individuals of his time. In one of his writings, he declared that, "man is the measure of all things—of those that are, that they are, and of those that are not, that they are not. ... With regard to the gods I know not whether they exist or not, or what they are like. Many things prevent our knowing; the subject is obscure, and brief is the span of our mortal life."

To twentieth-century sensibilities, it does not sound unreasonable. Even among true believers there is as likely to be sympathy for Protagoras's doubt as there is disdain for his infidelity. But this was the fourth century before Christ, when demons were real and monsters probable and even the most stable of societies existed in a chronic state of uncertainty—and what Protagoras had done was question the religion that was the groundwork of the entire Greek culture, its bulwark against the unknown. What he had done, in other words, was commit treason.

48

The Athenian assembly, summoned to consider the matter, censured Protagoras, ordering all who owned copies of his work to surrender them, whether the subject was agnosticism or something harmlessly unrelated. Officials collected the books and burned them in the marketplace, the flames leaping the height of Ionic columns, jittery flares of warning to all those who dared swerve from the path of orthodoxy. It was one of history's first bonfires of repression.

His many contributions to the Greek way of life now deemed inconsequential, Protagoras was banished from his homeland, commanded not to return. He set out for Sicily, but never got there. Perhaps he drowned on the way. For a period of time, misgivings about the reality of the Greek gods were submerged as well.

Plato did not shed tears over his fellow scholar's fate. There is no reason to think he wished Protagoras dead, but he likely thought that the Athenian assembly had been properly severe in destroying his books and exiling their author. Plato may have become a convert to the written word, but was discriminating about the uses to which it should be put. Like Solon, he believed that language that did not advance the purposes of the state, and their theological underpinnings, had no place being printed or uttered. In *The Republic,* Plato demanded of poets that they "stop giving their present gloomy account of the after-life, which is both untrue and unsuitable to produce a fighting spirit." In other words, if poems describe heaven as a place where the harps are out of tune and it always rains on weekends, what incentive is there for a reader or listener to risk being slain in battle for the glory of Greece?

Plato was especially vexed by the most illustrious of Greek bards, Homer. In 376 B.C., he urged that all Homerian works be cleansed of passages that might offend immature readers, passages in which, as Norwegian philosopher Jostein Gaarder has put it, "the gods resembled mortals too much and were just as egotistic and treacherous." In *The Odyssey,* for example, creatures of the spirit world are demeaned for their former status as human beings: "gibbering like bats that squeak and flutter in the depths like some mysterious cave when one of them has fallen from the rocky roof, losing his hold on his cluttered friends, with shrill discord the company set out."

Plato found this kind of thing irreligious, and turned up even more of it in *The Iliad*: "Ah then, it is true that something of us does survive even in the Halls of Hades, but with no intellect at all, only the ghost and semblance of a man."

If ignorance was the curse of humanity in ancient times, skepticism was the particular curse of the educated classes, a shadow cast by unreason over knowledge. So Plato believed, so he taught others. He could not understand such doubt as Homer expressed, and agreed with Solon that the only course was to eradicate it. Again from *The Republic*:

> Shall we therefore readily allow our children to listen to any stories made up by anyone, and to form opinions that are for the most part the opposite of those we think they should have when they grow up?
>
> We certainly should not.
>
> Then it seems that our first business is to supervise the production of stories, and choose only those we think suitable, and reject the rest. We shall persuade mothers and nurses to tell our chosen stories to their children, and by means of them to mold their minds and characters which are more important than their bodies. The greater part of the stories current today we shall have to reject.

It is a remarkable statement. Who would believe that the great philosopher from the land that cradled Western intellect could foreshadow a fundamentalist Christian housewife sitting at the kitchen table of her tract house in Wichita Falls, scribbling down the names of books that ought to be banned from the middle school library, and then stuffing the list into her pocketbook and heading off in a huff to the monthly meeting of the city council? Modern narrow-mindedness, ancient Greek roots.

But we are getting ahead of our story.

Now that the written tradition had overtaken the oral, the fear was no longer that printed language would erode the power of memory; it was that people would remember the wrong things, ideas to which they should not be exposed in the first place. The spoken word, after all, could be censored merely by silencing the speaker or forcing him to recant. It was a simple matter, often accomplished.

But language committed to paper had an existence independent of its source; silence the author and the page still prevailed, as if it were a living entity with its own means of carrying on. It could be confiscated, but this was a demanding and time-consuming task. It could be burned, but there might be other copies. The result was a threat to the established order like none it had ever known before. Attacks from hostile warriors it could repel; contrary ideas, freely expressed, were a foe with which it had no experience. Alarms were sounded and forces marshalled. The established order sprang into action.

In China it acted ruthlessly. Two hundred years after Plato, the Chinese undertook a search and destroy mission against the printed word, ruling that all books, regardless of content, were henceforth to be assigned to the imperial library, where they could be read only by scholars with a special permit. Volumes not deemed suitable for the library were to be brought to a central location and incinerated. Any person who came into possession of a stray manuscript was to hand it over. He was not to open it, not to skim a page or two, not even to bring the item into his home. "The penalty for withholding, reading or merely discussing a book," says C. V. Wedgwood in *The Spoils of Time,* "was forced labor or even death for the entire family of the culprit."

In the Occident, where literacy ran far less rampant, punishments were not so severe. With fewer people able to read, fewer books were manufactured to tempt them. And the situation did not seem likely to change in the foreseeable future, because even if the number of readers increased, there was no way for the number of books to keep pace. It could take as long as a year, for example, for the monks to put out a single copy of the Bible. Nor was there a means of making books affordable; it also took a year for a priest to earn enough money to buy himself the words of God, while most other citizens in the barter economies of the time could work their entire lives and never set aside enough to purchase a volume of any sort, sacred or otherwise. For these reasons, there was no regular state or ecclesiastical censorship of printed material in Europe until the sixteenth century.

But the seeds were sown midway through the fifteenth century, when came cataclysm, an explosion of the old ways, the Industrial Revolution of language. Johannes Gutenberg and Enrico Fermi have nothing in common, yet medieval authority regarded the one in much the same way that a later generation would regard the other; the printing press, like the split atom, seemed the release of a force so powerful, an energy so elemental, that it would resist all attempts by mortals to control it.

Not much is known of Gutenberg. There are question marks after the dates of his birth and death, and his biography is a record of conjecture as much as verifiable fact. But it is certain that in the vicinity of 1456, with the help of a young assistant named Peter Schöffer, Gutenberg invented molds that made printing from movable type feasible for the first time. It was a staggering achievement, requiring that the molds be adjustable to accommodate letters as wide as a "w" and as narrow as an "i"; that new metal alloys be developed to melt readily and as quickly cool; and that new kinds of ink be created, Gutenberg drawing his inspiration from Flemish painters who used linseed oil varnish as a base for their pigments.

Prior to this, Western man knew only block printing. This was the process of engraving an entire page of letters and numbers and symbols into a block of wood, which, once accomplished, meant that the page was formed for eternity; it could not be taken apart and composed into a different sequence of words, nor did it allow mistakes to be corrected easily.

Movable type changed all that. Suddenly books were produced more quickly and at less expense, and could be copied with greater ease than could block-printed volumes. For Gutenberg it was too late; he had devoted his life to the manuscript arts, and as a result of turning out so many books by hand, his eyes were ruined and his joints arthritic. But printers of the future would be spared his debilitating rigors, and readers of the future would find books much less difficult to come by.

At which prospect the church shuddered. It sensed the imminence of a chain reaction. In the thirteenth century, eyeglasses had been developed; by Gutenberg's time they were in fairly common use, which meant an increase not only in the number of people physically able to read, but in the number of hours per day and the number of days in a life that they could indulge their habit without strain. Now books were on the verge of becoming more accessible than ever. Now they were being published in the vernacular instead of just Greek and Latin, so that the interpretive skills of churchmen were not so necessary. Now the ranks of readers would swell, overflow. Call it supply-side literacy. A volume printed from movable type was still a costly item, and books would not be truly inexpensive until steam-powered presses were built in the nineteenth century. Still, the early presses made books relatively plentiful, and available in many cases to members of what we would today call the middle classes. "Beside the raskall multitude and the learned sages," said the English translator of Cicero's *Tusculan Disputations,* "there is a meane sort of men: which, although they be not learned, yet, by the quickness of their wits, can conceive al such poyntes of arte as nature could give."

But thanks to Gutenberg, they were about to be more learned than ever before. They were about to examine matters that had previously been foreign to them, making up their own minds, taking part in pocket rebellions against ignorance and tedium and injustice. Cataclysm indeed. If thinking for oneself were a material creation, a product of wood or stone or metal, its inventor would rank with Gutenberg himself, so radical an idea was it for most people of the time.

But how would they do that thinking? According to what guidelines? This is what had the church bracing for the worst. Would human beings reject the miracles and splendors recounted in the Bible because such tales were so far removed from the routine of their days, from the strenuous raising of crops and the thankless tending to animals? Or would they embrace the tales wholeheartedly, as escape routes from the very same lives of penury and hopelessness? Would they embrace them too much, missing the theological lessons and finding morals of their own? Would they deny the presence of morals altogether and merely read for amusement? Perhaps they would see the stately procession of words across the page, the elegant formation of them in their frozen choreography, as evidence not of the Almighty's genius, but of man's; and perhaps a writer, rather than continuing to think of himself as an intermediary between God and His creatures on terra firma, would decide to speak for himself, expressing his own beliefs and fears, doubts and desires. Perhaps instead of the writer just proclaiming and the reader just consenting, the two would join forces, collaborate. If so, on what?

And how would the reader respond when the writer openly expressed ideas contrary to those of the church? It is a question asked and then answered by Princeton scholar Robert Darnton of a later age. In *The Forbidden Best-Setters of Pre-Revolutionary France*, he writes,

> The physical qualities of the books reinforced their message in a way that may escape the perception of modern readers, who are used to seeing heterodoxy packaged and sold on the market. ... And the books had all the marks of respectability: frontispieces, title pages, prefaces, appendices, and notes. Unlike the unmanageable folio volumes of orthodox theology, still chained in some cases to shelves in draughty reading rooms, the little tomes of atheism could be carried in pockets and consulted in private. While their layout gave them an air of legitimacy ... their size made them seem designed to appeal to the realm of reason, where pros and cons could be pondered in the quiet of one's conscience.

The printing press, in other words, threatened anarchy. Within two decades of the first one, the papacy granted a license to the University of Cologne to punish those who wrote or read books that were "unauthorized." And Lorenzo de Medici's librarian thought that more such licenses would be necessary, and even then the presses would run amok. "You will put a hundred evil volumes into a thousand clumsy hands," he said, "and madmen will be loosed upon the world." So would geniuses, as a matter of fact, but the one was as frightening to the librarian and his notions of societal rectitude as the other.

For what Medici's man understood was that, although not literally weapons, books would inspire people to load and fire as surely as if their plots of land were under attack by marauders, and so would function as instruments of rebellion no less than of the status quo, of destruction as well as growth. The Bible, the Koran, the Torah, and other works of divine provenance have altered more lives for the better than all of history's enlightened rulers put together, and have led to the shedding of more blood than all the world's despots seeking enriched treasuries and bloated borders. They have toppled thrones, reorganized governments, and shifted alliances. They have denounced injustice, clarified misunderstanding, glorified decency, exposed duplicity, praised truth, and, in too many cases, sanctioned palpable falsehood for less than noble motives. They have made life bearable for those with no other choices, and beautiful for all who could accept the holy teachings without misgiving. Under the spell of scripture, readers have demanded that the values of their lords and prophets be recognized. The secular world has had no choice but to pay heed.

Give a man a hoe and he is something to exploit. Give him a book and he is something to fear.

In 1543, one of the presses made possible by Johannes Gutenberg printed a volume called *On the Revolutions of Celestial Spheres*. The author was an obscure cleric from Frauenburg, Poland, named Nicolaus Copernicus, who in addition to theology had been a student of law and medicine and various other subjects in his younger days. But the true calling of his spirit seems to have been the stars.

Up to that point in history, the principal religions of the world had taught that the earth was the center of the universe, with the sun and all other heavenly bodies revolving around it. Copernicus inverted the proposition. Even in notes he had made three decades before the publication of *Celestial Spheres,* he is unequivocal about the matter:

> 1. There is no one center of all the celestial circles or spheres. . . .
>
> 3. All the spheres revolve about the sun as their mid-point, and therefore the sun is the center of the universe. . . .
>
> 6. What appear to us as motions of the sun arise not from its motion but from the motion of the earth and our sphere, with which we revolve around the sun like any other planet.

His fellow astronomers were startled by Copernicus's findings, the very foundations of their science uprooted. But it was not just a challenge for them. With the earth in the universe's preeminent position, a solid basis existed for a theology that gave human beings a primary place in the galactic scheme of things, a theology whose major emphasis was on human thought, action, and comportment in the presence of the Almighty, as well as atonement for inherent mortal weakness. What was the Bible, after all, but the world's first how-to book, an instruction manual for the achievement of life ever-lasting through redemption of the soul?

But with humanity's home relegated to an inferior orbit in the heavens, so was humanity. As Will Durant wrote, "'When men stopped to ponder the implications of the new system, they must have wondered at the assumption that the Creator of this immense and orderly cosmos had sent His son to die on this middling planet. All the lovely poetry of Christianity seemed to 'go up in smoke' (as Goethe put it) at the touch of the Polish clergyman."

In time this view would change. In time a contrary argument, explained by Kirkpatrick Sale in *The Conquest of Paradise,* would take hold:

Far from reducing humans and their earth to an insignificant role in a sun-dominated solar system, it rather convinced the sixteenth-century European of the quite wonderful brilliance of the human mind and the beauty of its rationalism. "The new astronomy that seemed to reduce man to nothingness," as Egon Friedell points out, "made him in reality the unveiler, the seer, and even the legislator of the cosmos."

But that was in the future. For the present, Copernicus drew fire from all quarters, his name becoming a virtual epithet; other epithets descended on him without letup: heretic, monster, devil, fool, and charlatan. No one spoke more passionately against the father of heliocentrism than Martin Luther, who called Copernicus an "ass" and accused him of "trying to pervert the whole science of astronomy." Luther went on to settle the question of planetary motion once and for all, he assumed, by pointing out, "Sacred scripture tells us that Joshua commanded the Sun to stand still, and not the Earth."

Some of Copernicus's friends deserted him; many who knew of his ideas claimed ignorance, afraid of being tainted by mere awareness. There were demands for an apology, calls for execution, prayers to the effect that *On the Revolutions of Celestial Spheres* turn out to be a work of fiction.

The author, though, missed all the fuss. A man more concerned with the raw materials of truth than with its consequences, Copernicus may not even have sensed a storm was coming. One of the first copies of his book to roll off the presses reached him on his death bed. A friend handed it to him and watched him take it and with great care separate the covers. Copernicus is said to have "read the title page, smiled, and in the same hour died."

The book lived on in infamy. Early in the next century, Galileo roused the animus of the Inquisition, the Catholic Church's merciless crusade for orthodoxy, by publicly subscribing to the Copernican theory. "As to the arrangement of the parts of the universe," he had written to the Grand Duchess of Tuscany, "I hold the sun to be situated motionless in the center of the revolution of the celestial orbs, while the earth rotates on its axis and revolves around the sun."

Galileo was charged with blasphemy and put on trial. Ordered to renounce what his Inquisitors called "your grave and pernicious error and transgression," he complied, then was thrown into jail anyhow. It was a blow from which the esteemed scientist never recovered. "To have recanted was not considered a moral degradation," writes Giorgio de Santillana in *The Crime of Galileo.* "It was a deliberate *social* degradation, and it was as such that it broke the old man's heart."

On the Revolutions of Celestial Spheres broke records. It remained one of the top hits on the Catholic church's list of proscribed reading matter for more than two hundred years.

By Galileo's time, books of a secular nature almost surely outnumbered those that treated the gods. There was, after all, a Renaissance of classical learning in Europe, and it inspired volumes on philosophy and politics, history and commerce, geography and medicine, mathematics and biography, law and architecture, not to mention erotica, or, as Rousseau would later put it, "books that one reads with one hand." There were also, says historian Sir John Hale, "hundreds of books on social decorum . . . intended to suppress among the privileged their natural inclination to fart and brawl and thereby to blur painfully evolved social distinctions."

But it was books with religious content that incited the most Inquisitorial loathing, and responses were unfailingly prompt and extreme. In France, William Manchester reports, "the printing, sale or even the possession of Protestant literature was a felony; advocacy of heretical ideas was a capital offense; and informers were encouraged by assigning them, after conviction, one-third of the condemned's goods." Those who sold Protestant tracts might find themselves manning the oars as galley slaves. Those who transported the stuff were subject to fines and confiscation of cargo.

Similar penalties were enacted in Germany and Italy, and in Spain, where the excesses of the Inquisition were presided over by the fanatic monk, Tomás de Torquemada, physical torture often awaited the authors or readers of inappropriate books. "Sharp iron frames prevented victims from sleeping, lying, or even sitting," Manchester says in *A World Lit Only by Fire.* "Braziers scorched the soles of their feet, racks stretched their limbs, suspects were crushed to death beneath chests filled with stones." And with the execution of the bookman came the torching of his library.

The end of the Inquisition, a process that lasted for different lengths of time in different places, meant the end of barbaric retribution for contrary thought. What remained was the notion that the sole purpose of literature was to serve the ends of authority, secular and religious. The state, too, preferred the man with the hoe to one with the book, the former being more docile, the latter more likely to blame his king, rather than God or His earthly agents, for the meanness of life. God, after all, was *supposed* to work in mysterious ways; a mortal monarch, on the other hand, no matter how vile, ought at least to be comprehensible to his subjects. And just one bellyacher grousing about the crown on paper could be enough to rile a hundred other simplefolk whose grievances had previously been unarticulated. After all, says Robert Darnton, governmental power in Europe at this time did not generally come out of the barrel of a gun. Armies usually amounted to little more than a few companies of mercenaries and guards, police forces to a handful of constabularies. In order to impress their authority on the people, sovereigns acted it out—through coronations, funerals, royal entries, processions, festivals, fireworks, public executions. . . . But the dramaturgical form of power was vulnerable to insult. A well-aimed affront could puncture a reputation and destroy an entire performance.

And that was what a book could so easily be: a means of puncturing, a prelude to destruction. Darnton goes on to describe typical volumes of this kind, saying that they "purveyed a political folklore of dissolute kings and wicked ministers that, like the drip, drip of water on stone, wore away the layer of sacredness that made the monarchy legitimate in the eyes of its subjects."

For this reason, it was a crime to read, write, or own printed material harmful to the reputation of England's Queen Elizabeth or her court. It was also against the law to publish or import books thought to be blasphemous, which is to say, books that insisted on the supremacy of Roman Catholicism over the Church of England. Protestants had their Inquisitorial side, too.

But, unlike most peoples of the time, the English were willing to make distinctions. A man who read the wrong books might be a threat to society, but one who read correctly was perceived as an asset, and the English saw nothing incorrect in a fellow's perusing the Bible in the untutored solitude of his home. Maybe he would miss the point, but did that necessarily make him dangerous? Maybe he would pay too much heed to this or too little to that, maybe he would interpret too literally or not literally enough—but was the mighty crown of England to cower at so minor an offense? Besides, there was every reason to suppose that the raw intelligence the reader had newly begun to hone through his books would make him more amenable, not less, to the ratiocinations of his governing bodies.

So it was that in 1605, two brothers known to history only by their first names, William and Paul, broke into the residence of the Earl of Sussex. They were immediately apprehended—larceny in their hearts, lead in their boots, the old story. The brothers were tried, found guilty, and sentenced. The presiding magistrate said that because William made it a habit never even to open a book, he was to be hanged. Paul, being an occasional partaker of literary experience, was only to be tortured, perhaps by a branding of the thumb. Social historian Neil Postman explains that Paul "survived because he had pleaded what was called 'benefit of clergy,' which meant that he could meet the challenge of reading at least one sentence from an English version of the Bible. And *that* ability alone, according to English law in the seventeenth century, was sufficient grounds to exempt him from the gallows."

Postman further says that, in years following, the Bible-sentence defense became all the rage, something like temporary insanity or too many Twinkies today. In 1644, 203 men were convicted of capital offenses in the town of Norwich, and half of them pleaded benefit of clergy, "which suggests that the English were able to produce, at the very least, the most literate population of felons in history."

In the same year as the Norwich crime spree, the poet John Milton railed against censorship. Or did he? Said it was "as good almost [to] kill a man as kill a good book." But was it? Lamented the fact that "revolutions of acres do not oft recover the loss of a rejected truth." Except how was truth to be defined? In *Areopagitica,* which he called "A Speech for the Liberty of Unlicenced Printing," Milton says that books are not absolutely dead things, but do contain a potency of life in them to be as active as that soul was whose progeny they are; nay, they do preserve as in a vial the purest efficacy and extraction of that living intellect that bred them. . . .

We should be wary therefore what precaution we raise against the living labours of public men, how we spill that seasoned life of man preserved and stored up in books; since we see a kind of homicide may be thus committed . . . whereof the execution ends not in the slaying of an elemental life, but strikes at . . . the breath of reason itself, slays an immortality rather than a life.

It is hard to imagine words gathered in more eloquent, if baroque, assembly; hard to conceive of ideas expressed with greater fervency.

Yet Milton is almost as impassioned in the exceptions he allows to his indictment of censorship. He doubles back, in *Areopagitica,* to find obscenity contemptible, libel inexcusable, and atheism unworthy of a place on either page or tongue. In addition, citing the horrors of the Inquisition, he dismisses the Catholic Church as an institution of vast intolerance, and therefore undeserving of tolerance itself. He concludes by advising that "no book be printed, unless the printer's and the author's name or at least the printer's be registered. Those which otherwise come forth, if they be found mischievous and libelous, the fire and the executioner will be the timeliest and the most effectual remedy, that man's prevention can use."

It is as if Milton had written a stirring defense of pacifism, and then gone on to explain that war is justified on special occasions, say if your country wants more land or more gold or better-looking women or better-bred animals or it's a day of the week that ends in "y."

Part One: Distant Past

So deeply ingrained had the custom of bookbanning become in the two centuries since Gutenberg that even those who opposed it could not help but concede its occasional, if not frequent, necessity.

The Puritans did not flee from England so they could promote freedom of religion in Massachusetts Bay. Rather, they wanted to practice narrow-mindedness on their own terms. Unwelcome themselves on one side of the Atlantic, they became unwelcoming on the other. As Thomas Macaulay has suggested, the Puritans probably did not oppose the sport of bear-baiting because it was cruel to animals, but because it gave so much pleasure to spectators.

Like those who persecuted them at home, these overly pious, overly troubled souls refused to allow any challenges to their leaders, creeds, or books. The latter, in addition to the Bible in at least three languages, included Caesar's *Commentaries* and numerous volumes for children that taught numbers, the alphabet, and religion. To criticize these works was to subject oneself to the pillory, stocks, or dunking stool; to go so far as to rebel against them was to risk exile in the uncharted wilds of the New World.

Later English settlers in the southern colonies were no more open in their views. "I thank God we have not free schools nor printing," said the governor of Virginia in 1671, "and I hope we shall not have these hundred years. For learning has brought disobedience and heresy and sects into the world; and printing has divulged them and libels against the government. God keep us from both." And, he might have added, God keep us from the physical maladies attendant to reading. A century later, one J. G. Heinzmann wrote that the bibliophile's plagues included "susceptibility to colds, headaches, weakening of the eyes, heat rashes, gout, arthritis, hemorrhoids, asthma, apoplexy, pulmonary disease, indigestion, blocking of the bowels, nervous disorder, migraines, epilepsy, hypochrondia, and melancholy." It was believed by some that a person should not read after eating or while standing up. It was believed by others that a reader should take frequent breaks to quaff a healing libation.

So the British colonial experiment in North America did not start out as an experiment in unfettered communication; it was, rather, a means of expanding territory, opening new markets, and relocating undesirables. Even after the Revolutionary War, which was fought not only for the idea of freedom, but for the freedom of ideas—for the right of newspapers to dissect the character of public officials, of pamphlets to rail against the legislative actions of those officials, of books to question the existence of heavenly power or the wisdom of the church's manipulations on earth— even when the war was over and the United States of America stood as an accomplished fact, vestiges of suppression remained, like the ruins of a monument that has stood too long and too solidly to be time's complete victim. The censorship of unpopular beliefs continued as both custom and statute in the majority of New World communities; doubt in democratic precepts was not tolerated, support of the crown's previous policies not forgiven.

And in 1798, the Congress of the new nation passed something called the Sedition Act. More an attempt by John Adams's Federalists to gag Thomas Jefferson's Republicans than a measure of broader societal intent, the act nonetheless proclaimed that, "If any person shall write, print, utter or publish . . . any false, scandalous, and malicious writing or writings against the Government of the United States, or the President of the United States, with intent to defame the said Government, or either House of the said Congress, or the said President," that person might be imprisoned for two years and fined as much as $2,000.

Old habits not only died hard; they sometimes found themselves embedded in new legislation.

Yet a few months later, Jefferson and James Madison began pooling their efforts on what came to be known as the Kentucky and Virginia Resolutions, which found the Sedition Act unconstitutional. Other people and papers agreed, and the tide quickly turned. In 1801—after the prosecution of twenty-five writers, editors, and printers, ten of whom were convicted and sent to jail—the act expired. There were no protests about its demise, and no serious attempts to resurrect it. Americans seemed to lose interest in the vigilance required to maintain censorship.

As well they should have, and not just because they had cities to build, frontiers to expand, forests to clear, pastures to seed, institutions to found—an infant nation to nurture into adolescence. More to the point, the United States was a land created by ideas, founded on the printed page, "based on books and reading," as Daniel Boorstin has said. It did not follow the paths of so many other countries, evolving gradually through the millennia, with nomadic life giving way to settlement, savage behavior yielding to that of a more civilized nature, truculent northern tribes conquering complacent southerners and revitalizing the culture. Instead, the thirteen original colonies awoke one morning to find themselves the world's first instant republic: just add documentation. They were also the first country to came into being solely as a response to the successes and shortcomings of other lands; the former were incorporated in, and the latter omitted from, such seminal compositions as the Declaration of Independence, the Federalist Papers, the Constitution, the Northwest Ordinance, and the writings of Tom Paine, to name but a few—all of them turned out by men who had learned to write by learning first to read, and who had illuminated their own minds by starting out, in the later words of T. E. Lawrence, "following the light of another man's thought."

And it was not just the Founding Fathers who were beholden

to the printed page. So were farmers and smithies, explorers and roustabouts, women and children, who at about this time were beginning to make use of written language in an altogether different manner from their ancestors. As historian Rolf Engelsing explains, people were no longer reading "intensively"—in other words, they were no longer reading the same few books, like the Bible and an almanac, over and over, branding the contents onto their memories. Now they were reading "extensively"—exposing themselves to a variety of volumes, as well as newspapers and other periodicals. And they were reading them once, twice at the most, then moving on to the next publication that caught their eyes.

There was even one person who read "gastro-intestinally." Robert Darnton uncovered "the case of a woman . . . who 'ate a New Testament, day by day and leaf by leaf, between two sides of bread and butter, as a remedy for fits.' "

It is probably fair to say that the ability to read was as important to the average colonial citizen as the love of freedom; it may certainly be said that the one led to the other. In *Amusing Ourselves to Death,* Neil Postman tells us that "between 1640 and 1700, the literacy rate for men in Massachusetts and Connecticut was somewhere between 89 percent and 95 percent." The rate for women in the same colonies, Postman writes, "is estimated to have run as high as 62 percent in the years 1681–1697." In addition, Postman has found,

> Probate records indicate that 60 percent of the estates in Middlesex County [Massachusetts] between the years 1654 and 1699, contained books, all but 8 percent of them including more than the Bible. In fact, between 1682 and 1685, Boston's leading bookseller imported 3,421 books from *one* English dealer, most of these nonreligious books. The meaning of this fact may

be appreciated when one adds that these books were intended for consumption by 75,000 people then living in the northern colonies. The modern equivalent would be ten million books.

So there was neither desire nor justification for censorship in the United States of America. Fault-finders and freethinkers would be allowed their say here. Writers would be permitted to write regardless of their views, readers to read regardless of their inclinations, and the relationship between the two to develop however it would. This was not so much an endorsement of diversity as it was an expression of confidence that democracy was strong enough to withstand the assaults of even so powerful a force as a book.

That, at least, was how it seemed until well into the following century.

One of the most influential figures in the history of American censorship was not an American at all, but an Englishman with conscience enough to gird both sides of the Atlantic. By profession a doctor, Thomas Bowdler had a pragmatic turn of mind, and so had no sooner begun to consider the sins of literature than he realized that banning entire books was as demanding a task as eliminating entire strains of disease. So much labor, so little chance of success. He wondered about a path of lesser resistance. Could the part be excised instead of the whole, rather like a treatment of symptoms? Could the censor accomplish most of what he desired while at the same time seeming issue-oriented, not wild-eyed and vindictive? Bowdler answered in the righteous affirmative on both counts.

In the middle of nineteenth century and into the early twentieth, many American public schools taught the works of the world's most esteemed playwright from a ten-volume set called

The Family Shakespeare, the literary offspring of Bowdler and certain of his like-minded kin. They had toiled on it for years: reading the bard, reading *into* the bard, filtering the poetry of a lusty age through the sensibilities of one with a distinctive prissiness. The project's purpose, as Bowdler explained, was to remove from Shakespeare's oeuvre whatever material "cannot with propriety be read aloud in a family or is unfit to be read aloud by a gentleman to a company of ladies." He reminds us here of Plato, wanting to delete from Homer those passages that might offend young readers.

In *The Family Shakespeare,* the family Bowdler made more than a hundred cuts each in *Hamlet, Romeo and Juliet,* and *The Merchant of Venice.* Other plays suffered more radical surgery, still others less; none remained untouched by the censor's scalpel. Attorney William Noble, author of *Bookbanning in America,* provides the following example of dialogue that Bowdler sliced off the second scene of the third act of Hamlet:

Hamlet: Lady, shall I lie in your lap?
Ophelia: No, my lord.
Hamlet: I mean, my head upon your lap?
Ophelia: Aye, my lord.
Hamlet: Do you think I mean country matters?
Ophelia: I think nothing, my lord.
Hamlet: That's a fair thought to lie between maid's legs.
Ophelia: What is, my lord?
Hamlet: Nothing.
Ophelia: You are merry, my lord.

And although Shakespeare thought King Lear "every inch a king," Bowdler excised the description. *Every* inch? Surely you don't mean *those* inches?

Part One: Distant Past

To people of limited scope yet concern for appearances, Bowdler was a social reformer of the first rank, having devised a way to extirpate the lapses of the world's greatest authors while at the same time retaining most of the elements of their genius. Bertrand Russell's grandmother was among those to applaud. "I never can understand the objections to Bowdler," she wrote to her sister. "It seems to me so right and natural to prune away what can do nobody good. . . ." To H. L. Mencken, though, Bowdlerism was anything but natural. "Why print such bleeding fragments?" the iconoclast asked in a newspaper column in 1910. "As well attempt a condensed version of *The Critique of Pure Reason,* in words of one syllable: As well put the Constitution into couplets and Leviticus into limericks!"

Bowdler went on to publish a sanitized version of *The Rise and Fall of the Roman Empire,* and over the years countless others in positions of editorial responsibility, following his lead, have turned out literally thousands of different books, many of them the acknowledged classics of world literature, in formats specially retooled for the faint of heart and crabbed of outlook.

The practice continues today. Several textbook publishers reluctantly admit that they produce different editions of anthologies for different academic constituencies: more bad words in the New York copy than in Little Rock's, more sex in L.A. than in Omaha, more liberties with biblical interpretation in Minneapolis than in Tulsa. Attorney Noble writes that a "1980 Harcourt Brace Jovanovich edition of *Romeo and Juliet* [still widely used] . . . left out about ten percent of the text (while announcing they were omitting 'trivial or ribald wordplay and especially difficult, static passages of poetry.') Yet two-thirds of what was left out had sexual connotations."

Some of the rest had theological connotations:

70

When the devout religion of mine eye
maintains such falsehood, then turn tears to fire;
And these who, often drown'd, could never die,
Transparent heretics, be burnt for liars!

Such is the persistence of Bowdler's legacy, according to William Henry III in *In Defense of Elitism,* "that [textbook] publishers now employ more people to censor books for content that might offend any organized lobbying group than they do to check the correctness of facts." Such, also, is the present primacy of feelings over truth, appearances over accuracy.

Thomas Bowdler, one assumes, would have been proud. He was a resolute man, tireless, as diligent in his reading as a Ph.D. candidate preparing for orals. And as soulless as a bean-counter. He could not let his attention wander for an instant, he might miss a reference to the female anatomy. He could not look up, turn away; he might skip over insufficient adoration of the Almighty. Obsessed with parts, Bowdler never saw a whole book. Fixated on blemishes, he had no awareness of beauty; wallowing in fantasy, he had but the barest acquaintance with the real world, and the perspectives into which its doings could be placed by literature. He was dim-witted, high-minded, and short-sighted.

It paid off nicely for him. Bowdler's ceaseless striving after purer literary expression, his unrelenting attempts to infiltrate and neutralize the reader-writer cabal, resulted in his being honored by the language he helped to debase with elevation to the status of verb, transitive:

I bowdlerize.
You bowdlerize.
He, she, it bowdlerizes.
Shakespeare was bowdlerized.

Part One: Distant Past

Gibbon was bowdlerized.

Hemingway, Heller, and Vonnegut should have been bowdlerized.

Anthony Comstock became a noun. The third college edition of *Webster's New World Dictionary* says that the word "comstockery," probably coined by George Bernard Shaw in a fit of vituperation, means "ruthless suppression of plays, books, etc., alleged to be offensive or dangerous to public morals." The man himself looked every inch the definition's model. "A photograph of Comstock," writes the poet and critic Mark van Doren, "reveals a set of severely contracted facial muscles of the sort associated with acute conscience and the determination to exorcise sin from the whole of the subject's environment."

Like so many individuals who lived their lives large, Comstock started out small. His first forays into the reform of public morality consisted of advocating laws that penalized store owners for leaving naked dummies in their display windows overnight. They would excite men and embarrass women, Comstock believed, not to mention the effect they would have on children, arousing in them an unhealthy curiosity for the hidden secrets of flesh. Or plaster.

In 1873, when he was not yet thirty years old, Comstock led a frenzied lobbying campaign that resulted in an eponymous act by the United States Congress. It prohibited the mailing of "pornographic" materials, and made the term so broad that it even included birth control information of the most clinical variety. On the day President Ulysses S. Grant signed the act into law, its sponsor was exultant. "O how can I express the joy of my Soul or speak of the Mercy of God," he said. According to onlookers, there were tears in his eyes.

Comstock was able to parlay his legislation into a job as a special agent for the Post Office Department, and wasted no time

72

wreaking havoc on all who dared offend him, scorching the literary earth for miles around. The mere expunging of parts of books was not enough for Anthony Comstock; he set his sights on entire volumes, shelves, libraries. He wanted to bring down authors, raze publishing houses, demolish entire traditions, seeing to it "that there are no thistles or briars allowed to grow to wound and destroy childhood and youth as they pass by my beat." Comstock once bragged that in his first six months in the Post Office, he had seized 134,000 pounds of books. A quantity man was this sentinel at the gates of public piety, a thinker of bulk thoughts.

After a few months, Comstock organized the New York Society for the Suppression of Vice, a group whose motto was "Morals, not art or literature." It found little of the former in most of the latter. Comstock was disgusted by Mark Twain, offended by Herman Melville, puzzled at the least by Nathaniel Hawthorne. Bernard Shaw was "this Irish smut dealer"; French and Italian novels were "little better than histories of brothels and prostitutes, in these lust-cursed nations"; and Boccaccio's *Decameron* was "a wild beast," that Comstock would prevent "from breaking loose and destroying the youth of the land."

In fact, Comstock showed no patience for fiction from any pen. Scholar R. Laurence Moore has observed that with the development of the novel in the late eighteenth century came powerful Protestant opposition. It was not just the matter of bawdiness in Samuel Richardson, Henry Fielding and the like; it was the novel's "frank departure from 'truth,' and the pleasure it gave to readers by appealing to the free play of their imagination." Protestants worried about that kind of thing, where it would lead, how many might follow. Comstock worried more than most. Eventually, he would find something objectionable in virtually all the magnificent figures of world letters who would one day be known to a generation of academic nihilists as Dead White Males.

Part One: Distant Past

In *Intimate Matters,* their history of American sexuality, John D'Emilio and Estelle Freedman note that Comstock's targets "ranged from penny postcards sold on the Bowery to fine arts exhibitions in Fifth Avenue galleries depicting the nude boy, from dime novels of seduction to Leo Tolstoy's *Kreutzer Sonata,* an 1889 novel that spoke openly of prostitution. The conviction rate under the Comstock Act—as high as ninety percent of those accused—attested to Comstock's boundless (some claimed prurient) interest in suppressing vice."

D'Emilio and Freedman go on to claim a more brutal kind of efficiency for Comstock. They reveal that Ida Craddock, "a spiritualist who had published a guide to marital sex for women," was one of several suicides that resulted from Comstock's cold-blooded hectoring. Comstock himself put the total at fifteen, and without apparent remorse. In a letter written shortly before she died, Craddock verifies the role that the vice suppressor played in her fate: "Perhaps it may be that in my death more than in my life, the American people may be shocked into investigating the dreadful state of affairs which permits that unctuous sexual hypocrite, Anthony Comstock, to wax fat and arrogant, and to trample upon the liberties of the people, invading, in my own case, both my right to freedom of religion and to freedom of the press."

Here was a kind of censorship new to the ages, Bowdler and Comstock its advance guard. No longer was the purpose to justify the ends of church or state; the church in America has never been powerful enough to enforce a pervasive censorship, despite such gestures as the Roman Catholic Legion of Decency, and the state, for the most part, has had better things to do.

The new censorship, rather, reflected the wills of certain individuals: preachers and reformed tipplers and housewives too isolated from the world to judge its literary output; men whose starched white collars cut into their Adam's apples and women whose whalebone corsets cut off their circulation; persons who were highly motivated, deeply religious, and certain as Solon. "Jesus was never moved from the path of duty, however hard, by public opinion," said Comstock on one occasion, full of himself. "Why should I be?"

Encouraged by the freedoms of a democratic society to pursue their chosen ends, the new censors ignored the paradox that, in the process, they were denying others the right to their own pursuits. Comstock and Bowdler and those who followed in their wake believed that they could accumulate virtue as the robber barons accumulated capital, and were no less zealous in their quest. The result was that private impulses became public policy, one person's demons another's guiding principles. The new censors not only imposed their wills on friend and foe alike, but spread the canard that those who opposed them were tarnished by the very fact of their dissent. Specifically, they claimed that people who did not hold the same views as the censors were a threat not to the power of a particular institution, but to the ethical bedrock of the entire culture; by extension, all institutions would eventually topple, the civilization eroding from within. Altruism was the cloak of the new censorship, perhaps even its undergarment. Its goals, superficially considered, were nobler than those of the old: modesty, tastefulness, protection of the innocent. But its methods were, in their own ways, no less insidious.

Near the end of his life, Comstock sat with a reporter from the *New York Evening World* and looked back on the crusade to which his days had been devoted. He confessed to few regrets, no significant misjudgments. Surveying the wreckage, he found only growth. He told the reporter that his efforts on behalf of sterilized literature had "convicted persons enough to fill a passenger train of sixty-one coaches, sixty coaches containing sixty passengers each and the sixty-first almost full." Estimated total weight of destroyed books, magazines, and pamphlets: 160 tons.

Part One: Distant Past

What does one make of a man like this? How does one go about finding an essence, a closer link to humanity than seems apparent on the surface? It does no good to describe Comstock as fundamentally decent, for it misses the larger point that decency gone haywire is an evil no less than the normal strains of same. It does no good to describe him as sincere, since the word also applies to people as diverse in their actions as George Armstrong Custer, Mary Baker Eddy, and Diamond Jim Brady. It does no good to call him greedy; financial gain was at best a minor consideration for Comstock, even though the Society for the Suppression of vice got 50 percent of the fine for each conviction brought about by its vigilantism. And there is no reason to point out that Comstock was the child of parents who descended directly from the Massachusetts Bay Puritans, the modern variety of which would later be dismissed by H. L. Mencken as people who harbor "the haunting fear that someone, somewhere may be happy." It might all be true, but that does not make it sufficient; Comstock's motivations, like those of all truly outer-directed persons, must remain, at least in part, a mystery.

In their biography of the reformer published in 1927, Heywoud Broun and Margaret Leech confess their own puzzlement, finding details of Comstock's early life sketchy, and explanations for his deeds never entirely clear. They write, "It is true that he was passionately devoted to his mother and to her memory, that as a lad he trapped animals and shot robins, that he collected postage stamps down to the day of his death, that he was skillful at fine cabinet work, and that he loved the graceful curved lines of Japanese vases and filled his house with these trinkets."

But if there was a substantive clue to the inner man in such a mass of unrelated detail about the outer life, it escaped the notice of the authors.

I wish it were not so. I wish I knew more about Anthony Comstock, starting with how he arrived at his definition of propriety and then extended it into a code of enforcement and finally a lifelong obsession. Was he scarred by obscenity as a child? Broun and Leech found no evidence of it. Was he browbeaten by parents, curdled by friends and associates? Was there no one with whom he could have discussed life and art, no one who could have helped?

Most of all, I would like to know whether Comstock really meant it when, on November 8, 1864, several months shy of his twenty-first birthday, he wrote in his diary, "Spent part of day foolishly as I look back, read a Novel part through." Did he ever read a novel, or any other book, all the way through? Except for that day, did he even pick up a book at all without looking for an excuse to send the author to jail? Did he ever want to be a fictional character or go to a fictional place, if only for a while? Did he think longingly of a Bret Harte or a James Fenimore Cooper hero? A Henry David Thoreau or Herman Melville locale? Did he ever close his eyes, young Anthony Comstock, and soar away from the confines of a summer evening into a purple sky—circling Big Ben, darting behind a church spire, ducking under a cloud shaped like an elephant's head?

Did he ever leave the ground in more modest fashion? Did he ever get up on his tiptoes?

If not, I feel sorry for him.

If so, how could he have loaded so many people onto those train cars?

In 1914, the year before Anthony Comstock died of "overdoing in a purity convention," as Broun put it, a man named James Joyce, who could make crazily hypnotic rhythms—if not always perfect literal sense—out of language, started writing the novel *Ulysses*.

In 1918, a literary magazine called *The Little Review,* edited by Margaret Anderson and Jane Heap, printed the first excerpt.

Part One: Distant Past

In 1921, on the basis of this and other chapters appearing in small circulation periodicals, the New York Court of Special Sessions found Joyce's work-in-progress to be "unintelligible" and "obscene," making it the first book in the history of the United States to be censored before it was published.

In 1922, a limited edition of *Ulysses,* brought out in Paris, became the rage among roving bands of European intellectuals and their American hangers-on. According to authorities on this side of the Atlantic, the book was not suitable for import. Guards were posted, parcels carefully checked.

From 1923 to 1932, copies of Joyce's novel were smuggled into the United States as if they were bottles of bootleg hooch, their illegal pleasures to be savored in corners of society where the law did not look, among friends of similar persuasion.

Also from 1923 to 1932, shipments of the book intended for American readers were confiscated in London, Mexico, and Windsor, Ontario, among other places. Boxloads that made it across American borders were nabbed in Chicago, New York, Boston, and at least half a dozen other large cities. Four hundred books here, five hundred there, two or three or another hundred somewhere else. They added up. Throughout the Roaring Twenties, there were more copies of *Ulysses* under lock and key than there were in the open.

In 1933, as a result of a suit brought by Random House, the American publication of Joyce's classic was finally permitted. U.S. District Court Judge John Woolsey conceded that there was "an unusual frankness" to the book; nonetheless, he did "not detect anywhere the leer of the sensualist. I hold, therefore, that it is not pornographic."

For the next two decades, there is little to say about the banning of books in America—or rather much to say, but little that sheds new light on the relationship among readers and writers and those who would keep them apart. A few books were censored in this place because of sex, a few in that place because of religion. There were some cases of groups protesting a suggestive picture on a dust jacket, other cases of a group up in arms about dirty words in the text. Maybe a criminal act in a book was portrayed too graphically and thought to have inspired a crime in real life; maybe life itself was portrayed as too nasty and brutish and short. There were books that raised questions about the efficacy of various social and governmental institutions in the wake of the Depression; some people tried to halt their publication. There were books that forced a reappraisal of the natures of patriotism and commerce in the wake of World War II; some people thought such views unfit to print.

Attempts at censorship, though, when they happened at all, broke out randomly, like brush fires, and were often as quickly extinguished. No new trends were discernible, no movements seemed to be building. The country was otherwise occupied, and there was a sameness to the censors' cries that worked against them.

But when the Second World War ended, the uneasy union between the United States and the Soviet Union grew quickly uneasier. Alger Hiss was an accused spy, Klaus Fuchs an admitted one, and Julius and Ethel Rosenberg were actually put to death for giving away U.S. secrets. The Soviet Union, recipient of information treacherously obtained and passed by the saboteurs, dropped an Iron Curtain over Eastern Europe, as if to safeguard the apocalyptic new technologies now in its arsenal.

The man who behaved like a Soviet ally in the Orient, Chairman Mao, overran mainland China with his instantly replenishable army of millions, and drove the American puppet, Chiang Kai-shek, to early retirement on an offshore island. Who lost

China? the right wing wanted to know. Who said it was ours to lose? countered the left. But suddenly there were doubts: what really happened at Yalta? Charges: our government sold us out at Potsdam. Revisions of history: Harry Truman brought so many Alger Hisses into the State Department that they could have had their own football team.

And the Truman Doctrine was a call to arms for people with one set of views, while the Marshall Plan was capitulation for those with another. The Berlin blockade was an act of provocation, the airlift a show of brinksmanship. War erupted in Korea and hysteria followed at home, with the one igniting the other and the mushroom cloud now no longer the exclusive stuff of nightmares, but of nagging apprehensions at high noon. So many bomb shelters were built so quickly and of such uniform appearance that you'd have thought Bill Levitt, the tract-home mogul, was behind them. Americans laid in canned goods and listened for sirens and, on Saturday afternoons, ventured to movie theaters to purge themselves on double features about huge, scaly monsters created by atomic energy gone berserk.

A man who worked for the government, a policy planner in the State Department named George Kennan, had a solution. He called it containment. It meant learning to live with the devil. The devil's name, as everyone knew, was communism. The name of the devil who rose up to fight it on behalf of the United States of America was Sen. Joseph R. McCarthy, Tail Gunner Joe, Republican of Wisconsin and the free world.

McCarthy was a man of extraordinary vision. He could see communist influence everywhere, in places where others could not even detect political ideology. The State Department incubated communism, the academy taught it, and the publishing industry spread it like a plague bacillus, with historians writing of its inevitability and novelists of its promise, poets of its blessings and essayists of its logic, agriculturalists of its bountiful yields. This is what McCarthy believed. Or what he professed to believe. Or what he made up in so many little white lies and big black jokes to get his name in the papers and his mug on the newsreels. Due process was the greatest victim of the senator's rampaging ism, but books were no less in the crosshairs of his misguided weaponry.

In some cases, it was McCarthy himself who demanded that printed material be censored, personally summoning to his office or hearing room authors, editors, and officials of the International Information Agency. He would vilify them for their views and assail their loyalty and sanity. He would pound desktops and threaten Armageddon, reserving special abuse for those whose reports on foreign affairs and domestic disintegration carried too light a cargo of anticommunist invective. "He was a master of the scabrous and the scatological," says Richard Rovere, in *Senator Joe McCarthy*, "his talk laced with obscenity. He was a vulgarian by method as well as, probably, by instinct." Men and women alike were known to stagger out of their sessions with McCarthy in tears, sometimes contemplating anesthetization by alcohol, other times suicide, in the wake of the shattering of their psyches.

But McCarthy also fulminated against writers who, while eschewing politics as a topic, were, in the senator's view, sympathetic to the goals of communism in their personal lives. Or at least not as unsympathetic as he thought robust, red-blooded Americans ought to be. For this reason, removed from the shelves of government-sponsored libraries at home and abroad were volumes by Dashiell Hammett, Howard Fast, and most remarkably, Rhea Foster Dulles, cousin of one of the most aggressive red-haters of the period, John Foster Dulles, secretary of state under Dwight Eisenhower. Also relegated to scrap heaps and bonfires were an assortment of works by Mark Twain, suspected of tinting pink despite the fact that he died in 1910 and the revolution did not transform Russia until 1917.

Meanwhile, private citizens, steamrollered by the zeitgeist, began thinking like McCarthyite censors without awaiting the master's direct cue. Often this required great leaps of imagination. Was John Steinbeck too sensitive to certain items on Moscow's agenda? *The Grapes of Wrath* preached the overthrow of capitalism. Did Gordon Parks think that life in the United States tended to be a more difficult proposition for people of dark skin than for those of light? *The Learning Tree* would pollute the minds of all who read it. Did Arthur Miller express too much doubt about the wisdom of nuclear confrontation? Willy Loman was in bed with Uncle Joe Stalin.

And then, just when it seemed that the self-servingly ignorant had scaled all remaining summits of literary misunderstanding, along came a housewife from Indiana named Mrs. Thomas J. White. Cue the kazoos, strike up the washboards. Dear Mrs. White somehow got it into her head that the nearby school should stop teaching, or even making reference to, the notoriously left-leaning brigand of Sherwood Forest. "There is a Communist directive in education now to stress the story of Robin Hood," Mrs. White announced one day, never bothering to reveal the source of her intelligence. "They want to stress it because he robbed the rich and gave to the poor. That's the Communist line. It's just a smearing of law and order."

Alarms were also raised in other communities about the political affiliation of the Merry Men's leader, with politicians hinting at it in their speeches, editorial writers prattling about it in their columns. But even in times as paranoid as these, the matter seemed more of a molehill than an issue. Rebuttals came from near and far. In fact, says Richard Fried in his history of the McCarthy period, *Nightmare in Red,* "The current sheriff of Nottingham, no less, protested the smear on Robin's good name."

A bad name is what McCarthy gave anticommunism. A worse one was his gift to censorship. Bowdler could perhaps be defended, or at least explained, on the grounds of a legitimate interest in the budding of young minds. Comstock could be explained, however flimsily and incompletely, as having had a genuine concern for the moral fiber of society. But McCarthy was an opportunist, pure and simple and vile. His craving for self-promotion at the expense of fairness was apparent even to some of his supporters. In *McCarthy and His Enemies,* basically an apologia, William F. Buckley, Jr., and L. Brent Bozell concede that his fellow members of the United States Senate should have censured McCarthy long before they actually got around to it.

He was correct, of course, in assuming that there is a connection between what an author believes and what he writes; in most cases, the former is the motivation for the latter. But McCarthy proceeded from there to the position that a book should be tossed from its stall in the marketplace of ideas if an author accepts even a few of the premises of an unpopular political philosophy, and that was a harkening back to attitudes medieval, when readers and writers were regarded as bands of plotters, their methods selfish if not nefarious, their goal to tear down the pillars of church or state or both, merely to glory in the wreckage.

Such attitudes would not infest the country again until Ronald Reagan was elected president in 1980, and fundamentalist Christians, who had long believed that the gates of heaven welcomed them, now assumed that the door to the Oval Office had swung wide as well.

According to various library associations, more attempts to censor books were made during the Reagan years than during any other decade of the century. Fundamentalists were the instigators in most cases, and some of their arguments were so absurd that the debate over Robin Hood, by contrast, seemed worthy of being held at the Oxford Union and moderated by Bill Moyers.

What follows are some of the books and stories that fundamentalist groups have tried to evict from school and community libraries in recent times, as well as summaries of their reasons. Several of the latter are excerpted from Joan Delfattore's excellent study, *What Johnny Shouldn't Read,* and a few others from Russell Jacoby's *Dogmatic Wisdom.*

Lysistrata, Aristophanes. The decision of the women of Greece to withhold sex from their husbands until they promise to stop waging war is vulgar, and worse, contributes to the "promotion of women's lib."

The Red Badge of Courage, Stephen Crane. Fails to acknowledge the occasional necessity of war.

Hiroshima, John Hersey. Marginally acceptable, as far as it goes, in depicting the horrors of war in the nuclear age, but too one-sided. It "should be balanced by an account of the bombing of the *Arizona.*"

Hamlet, William Shakespeare. The appearance of the ghost of the title character's father contradicts Christian doctrine, which holds that there are no such things as ghosts, except the Holy One.

Romeo and Juliet, William Shakespeare. The fate of the young lovers encourages teenagers to kill themselves if their problems seem more than they can handle.

A Modest Proposal, Jonathan Swift. Tempts the people of Texas, in times of excessive hunger, to consider the consumption of their fellow human beings, especially young, tender ones.

"Benjamin Franklin Flies His Kite," author unknown. The story, in various seventh grade readers, quotes Franklin's epitaph, which says:

The Body of
B. Franklin, Printer,
Like the cover of an old Book,
Its Contents torn out,
And stript of its Lettering & Gilding,
Lies here, Food for Worms.
But the Work shall not be lost;
For it will, as he believ'd,
Appear once more
In a new and more elegant Edition
Corrected and Improved
By the Author.

Thus, "Benjamin Franklin Flies His Kite" reveals that the Founding Father believed in reincarnation and was therefore a Hindu.

The Autobiography of Benjamin Franklin. Reinforces the man's un-Christian leanings.

The Wizard of Oz, Frank Baum. The Tin Man, the Cowardly Lion, and the Scarecrow become, respectively, more caring, courageous, and intelligent without resort to prayer, which is an unrealistic means of acquiring virtue. Further, the book "promotes Satanism," because Dorothy is aided in her adventures by the good witch, Glenda.

"To Build A Fire," Jack London. The author implies that the main character in this short story could have saved his life had he made better use of his wits when trapped in the wilds. Said a plaintiff in a court case against the tale: "Man's survival does not depend upon man's ability to create in his imagination solutions to his problems. Man's survival is determined by God."

"Freddy Found a Frog," Alice James Napjus. The title character in this second grade tale is opposed to suggestions that his amphibian be cooked or used as bait for fish. This, said some fundamentalists, contributes to "an excessively empathetic, pantheistic, non-Christian, nonutilitarian view of animals."

All stories that refer to Santa Claus or the Easter Bunny or the Tooth Fairy. They lure children away from organized religion into the worship of fantasy creatures instead of God Almighty.

All Tarzan adventures, Edgar Rice Burroughs. Bad enough that the ape man lives with Jane out of wedlock. Worse that he never acknowledges the sin or even wrestles with his conscience about it.

All works of Edgar Allan Poe. He was a cocaine addict.

All works of Oscar Wilde. He was a homosexual.

All works of James Baldwin. He, too, was a homosexual, and a rabble-rouser besides.

"Goldilocks and the Three Bears," traditional. The little girl is an unrepentant crook, having committed illegal entry, petty larceny of porridge, and vandalism of Baby Bear's stool.

"Jack and the Beanstalk," traditional. Jack's attitude toward the giant teaches disrespect for persons in positions of authority.

The Stupids Step Out, Harry Allard and James Marshall. It portrays "families in a derogatory manner and might encourage children to disobey their parents."

A Light in the Attic, Shel Silverstein. One of the poems in this collection "encourages children to break dishes so they won't have to dry them."

Sister Carrie, Theodore Dreiser. Too negative.

The Diary of Anne Frank. Too sad.

The Adventures of Huckleberry Finn, Mark Twain. Too cynical about organized religion, and guilty as well of the "glorification of moral independence."

At which charge H. L. Mencken would have guffawed into his lager. Mencken regarded Twain's opus as the great American novel, and the author as "the true father of our national literature, the first genuinely American artist of the blood royal." And Ernest Hemingway, not noted for his gracious assessments of other writers, agreed. "All modern literature," he once opined, "comes from one book by Mark Twain called *Huckleberry Finn.*"

Yet the history of attempts to ban the volume is a striking one; fundamentalist Christians were hardly the first, nor were acolytes of the lamentable McCarthy. Over the years, *The Adventures of Huckleberry Finn* has been seen as a cornucopia of literary crimes and misdemeanors, a paean to moral turpitude and social anarchy, all things to all censors. In fact, it might well be the most reviled book in the history of American letters.

Shortly after its publication in 1885, Twain's novel was denounced for its mocking depiction of the Victorian work ethic, its denigration of formal schooling, and the author's apparent belief that if a person finds a law immoral, he is within his rights to disobey it. Some people objected to the book's loopy syntax, which seemed to ridicule the foundations of rational thought, while others decided that Twain had abrogated his role as a creative artist and merely reworked his previous book about Huck's pal Tom Sawyer, repeating characters and setting and themes. When *Century* magazine printed an excerpt, it eliminated all references to nudity and dead cats. And, of course, there were charges that an account of a white boy and a black man getting along famously, even if fictitiously, was not in the best interests of a well-ordered society.

Yet in recent years, it is the victims of racism, not its perpetrators, who have objected to Huck's relationship to the slave Jim. In 1957, the black writer Ralph Ellison said that "Jim's friendship with Huck comes across as that of a boy for another boy rather than as the friendship of an adult for a junior; thus there is implicit in it not only a violation of the manners sanctioned for relations between Negroes and whites, there is a violation of our conception of adult maleness."

This continues to be the opinion today among believers in what is called political correctness, a system of thought whose basic assumption is that the First Amendment is just kidding, or else that its protections are to be so selectively bestowed that one needs a rulebook in a looseleaf binder to determine who qualifies for them and who does not. Slide a few pages in according to today's whim; slide a few out according to the cultural gestapo of tomorrow.

Take the case of the man in Fairfax, Virginia—an administrator at the Mark Twain Intermediate School, no less!—who called *The Adventures of Huckleberry Finn* "the most grotesque example of racism I've ever seen in my life." One wonders whether the fellow ever heard of a lynching.

At other schools in the Fairfax environs, the book has been pushed back to older grades, which seems reasonable; has been shifted from required reading to an elective, which is irresponsible; and has in some cases been banished altogether as parents, educators, and bureaucrats put their heads together and tried to decide what to make of it, which is even more irresponsible. At prestigious St. Albans, a private school for boys in Washington, D.C., Huck and friends recently had a two-year sabbatical, the result of which is that the book will probably return to the curriculum in the fall of 1995 as an elective for juniors and seniors. The decision has been applauded by some, cursed by others. Bill Matory has done both. A seventeen-year-old senior at St. Albans in the fall of 1994, Matory, who is black, does not understand why *The Adventures of Huckleberry Finn* was not an option in *his* junior and senior years. "It's like taking a big part of America's past away from us," he told the *Washington Post.* "As an African American male, you must understand why the book was written and how it was written. And we are smart enough to understand that."

According to Delfattore, the politically correct are second only to the religiously correct as censors of books in the United States in the 1990s. One group is secular in orientation, the other religious; one resides on the ideological left, the other on the right; one is accused of ushering in the timid new world; the other of spreading bigotry and hatred. The two share nothing in the way of philosophy, everything in the way of approach.

It is a sad irony of the present time that the power of literature is acknowledged more by those who fear it than by those who find it inspiring. Where is the society that memorializes Sir James M. Barrie for his contributions to human flight? What chorus sings the praises of Ayn Rand for the praises she herself sang to the glory of the unshackled human spirit? Who meets in regular session to pay homage to Marcus Aurelius for teaching that valor and decency can reside in the same human breast?

If, as Ezra Pound has said, literature is "news that stays news," why are Flaubert and Balzac not on the front pages of newspapers, Hardy and Dickens not on the covers of magazines, E. B. White and Truman Capote not on the tips of tongues where reasonable men and women congregate? Why not Anne Tyler on "Nightline," "20/20" looking clearly at John Le Carré, "48 Hours" devoting at least that much time to Doris Kearns Goodwin? "When we started out," says Kurt Vonnegut, referring to the early writing days of Irwin Shaw and James Jones and Norman Mailer and himself, "one story in *The New Yorker* like 'Franny and Zooey' would have people talking from coast to coast, or one Ray Bradbury story in the *Saturday Evening Post.* Then, you could write a story or a novel that would knock someone's block off. We were focused. There is no such focus anymore."

How many people know that Niccolo Machiavelli manages to hold cabinet rank in the minds of astute politicians even though he has been dead for several centuries? How many know that Karl von Clausewitz remains an honorary field marshall to military leaders of breadth and vision? How many know that when Abraham Lincoln met Harriet Beecher Stowe, author of *Uncle Tom's Cabin,* he referred to her as the "little lady" who "made" the Civil War? Does anyone care that Edith Wharton's portraits of society have lost none of their hues or textures, or that George Orwell's rages against injustice maintain their original astuteness? Would anyone even believe that in the 1920s, when Americans were asked to name the ten greatest figures in all of history, they chose four writers among them? Shakespeare, Dickens, Tennyson, Longfellow—all were nominated for the ages, newsmakers who stayed newsmakers. Today, they are lucky to be Final Jeopardy answers.

In some parts of the country, among some kinds of people, books seem to be taken to court more often than they are to heart, and the critical reader is like the health inspector tramping through a greasy spoon; both are looking for violations of code; neither expects to find anything worthy of consumption, much less of nutritional value.

The attitude is a mystery. Believing that the Almighty exercises total control over human life, fundamentalists should find the rantings of a mere author inconsequential. Believing that a democracy provides equal rights and privileges for all, the politically correct should favor the airing of all points of view, anticipating the victory of reason. Right and left alike should concede that even books of malevolent intent have a purpose—if nothing else, to instruct the reader in the ways of malevolence, and to assist him, however inadvertently, in the preparation of a defense. Yet such is not the case. The right is afraid of licentiousness; the left cannot bear incivility. Literature is caught in the middle, and those who evaluate it for the public schools grow ever more timid.

*   *   *

A decade and a half ago, as a correspondent for NBC News, I reported on a fundamentalist bookburning in a small town in the Midwest. A local church sponsored the event, but had little support from other churches or neighboring communities or even, it seemed to me, from the majority of people in the town itself. Most of them went along with the idea of a literary exorcism by fire, but few seemed ardent about it, and fewer still provided me with the kind of damnation-and-brimstone sound bites I was expecting.

It had been 2,400 years since the various works of Protagoras were ignited in the heart of Athens.

The story took two days to shoot, my crew and I taping the actual bookburning, for which a zoning variance had to be granted; interviews with a dozen or more people on both sides of the issue; and scenes of daily life in the town, context for the conflagration. We shot farmers working their fields, salesclerks tending their counters, mechanics fixing cars, barbers giving haircuts and slapping on bay rum by the palmful, and old-timers on the stone bench in front of City Hall, spitting tobacco juice onto the sidewalk and resolving matters both momentous and trivial as they spoke to one another so desultorily that they might have been using code.

In the course of it all, I got to know some of the fundamentalists reasonably well. I forgave them their reputation; they forgave me my affiliation with the Eastern liberal media establishment. One man, the vice president of the local bank, for which he had begun to work as a part-time teller almost a quarter of a century earlier, told me that life was good in his town and he hoped my piece would show it. The unemployment rate was below the national average, the number of alcoholics small, the air clean. The kids, he said, did not use drugs or copulate promiscuously. "They're fine young people, Mr. Burns. You'll see."

Part One: Distant Past

The next night, the crew and I taped one of the families that had organized the bookburning as they got dressed for the big do: sweaters and sweatshirts to protect themselves from the evening chill, T-shirts and jerseys underneath so they could take off the outer garments if the flames got too hot. "We think we've got something special here," said the sister-in-law of the bank vice president; she was shooing her husband and kids out the door, into the station wagon, bound for duty. "Not flashy, but special."

I nodded.

"We're just trying to hang on."

It was one of those station wagons with faux wooden panels on the sides and a name like Suburbanite or Country Squire. It eased out the driveway and down the street and, before it disappeared around the stop sign on the corner, one of the kids rolled down a back window and waved.

I waved back.

Within two hours the fire in the church parking lot was raging like the blast furnaces of Protestant hell. Blue-orange flames shot into the night, plastering themselves against an almost starless sky, as volume upon volume of incinerated literature snapped, crackled, and hissed below. Two teenage boys did their best to keep up with the demand for tinder, but it was no easy task. They loaded their wheelbarrows with books in the church basement and pushed them across the parking lot with the wheels squeaking and the huge mounds of cargo constantly shifting, threatening to topple. Sometimes a novel or a biography or an anthology of poems would fall and the boys would kick it aside, picking it up on their next trip and adding it to the mountain of condemned tomes they were erecting about twenty feet from the inferno's outer edge.

As for those who actually threw the books into the blaze, several of them had to be restrained; they wanted to make the flames soar so high that they might have gotten out of control, endan-

92

gering nearby buildings and eliminating forever the possibility of a future zoning variance. A few small children, the spirit willing but the forearms weak, stood on the perimeter of the fire and flung books so far short that they had to be pushed the rest of the way by an old man with a rake, who seemed to be playing a peculiarly listless version of shuffleboard.

"How tight can you get with that lens?" I said to my cameraman.

"How tight do you want me to get?"

I held one hand parallel to the ground halfway up my nose and the other parallel to the ground at the mid-point of my forehead. "The frame like this."

He shook his head. "I'd have to be right up in their faces."

I told him to do it.

"It bugs people sometimes, I move in like that."

"I don't think they'll even notice."

He shrugged.

I wanted their eyes. What I saw in them that night, and was determined to capture on tape, was something at once primitive and reverential. They were wide, unblinking, either focused on something deep within the flames or not focused at all; either as intense as lasers or as blank as television screens when the sets are turned off. So many pairs of eyes, so many tentacles of fire, so much crackling of burnt books in the air.

I tried to decide what the eyes reminded me of, who they seemed to belong to. Was it cave dwellers, their awe inspired by the blaze's violent majesty? Was it Ku Klux Klanners, the full depths of their hatred unleashed by the heat and frantic flickering? Was it pyromaniacs, their aesthetic impulses triggered by the perversely poetic dance of fire and sparks in the breeze?

No, I decided after a few minutes; it was none of these. What the people at the bookburning in the small midwestern town reminded me of was not other human beings at all. It was animals. Small animals. Cats. Maybe kittens. Attractive creatures: cute, cuddly, fun to play with. I could imagine myself living next door to them and getting along just fine when we happened across one another on the street: a nod and a stroke from me, from them a flick of the tail and a rumbling purr.

But kittens are too insecure to behave sensibly when threatened, and too unsophisticated to understand what really constitutes a threat. At perceived danger they bare teeth, scratch, and claw. Backs arch, eyes gleam with malignant light. They are afraid of whatever is out of their direct ken, and when you are a small animal in a large cosmos, so very much is. They were drawn to the fire, terrified of the fire, kin to the fire; it seemed to fill them with longing as it drained them of reason.

I watched. The cameraman shot them in extreme closeup. Overhead, a shooting star drew a white line under the moon.

I wanted to say something to the men and women feeding the flames. I've read some of the books you're cremating, is how I might have begun, and there's no point. They won't hurt you. The guy who wrote *Slaughter-House Five* has as good a heart as you do, is just as sentimental in his way. The guy who wrote the *Rabbit* novels is lamenting the rootlessness of his character's life, not advocating it. Sure, the woman who wrote *The Women's Room* is angrier than you, but does that mean you reject her reasons without a hearing, consign her arguments, like her prose, to flames of oblivion?

I wanted to say: Read *Catch-22* more slowly; it celebrates the human spirit in times of adversity no less than you do with your faith. Read *Native Son* more openly; it lashes out at injustice precisely as you would if you had been its victims. Read *Lord of the Flies* more carefully and *One Flew Over the Cuckoo's Nest* less defensively and *Ordinary People* without taking it as some kind of personal indictment. Get to know the people who populate the books. Walk the roads they walk and smell the air they breathe and, if you can, feel the pains inflicted on them, or the pains they inflict on others. You don't have to agree with the characters or with the authors who sired them, but you should try to understand their worlds. It is better that possibilities be raised and rejected than that they never be raised at all.

I wanted to say: I know that a lot of these books are not appropriate for your children, but keep your children away from them until they're older. Don't burn them. Don't teach violence against ideas. Teach the testing of ideas, the competition among them, the struggle to find the viable ones and put them into practice. Teach your disagreement with the ideas you do not find viable, and explain your reasons. But don't teach fire. "The great threat to the young and pure in heart," said Heywood Broun in his biography of Anthony Comstock, "is not what they read, but what they don't read."

I wanted to say to the men and women in the church parking lot: Be parents, not arsonists. I wanted to say: Nice kitty. I opened my mouth a time or two, closed it as quickly, spoke not a word.

Then I turned away from the bookburning that I was covering for NBC News, but I could not escape the flames. They were reflected in the windows of a small restaurant across the street, the panes of ebony glass shimmering like a sheet of liquid metal. I could still hear the books sizzling, and as the wind shifted I smelled a particularly acrid kind of smoke.

I stuffed my notebook into my pocket and closed my eyes for a moment. In the next instant I heard a pitchpipe. My eyes snapped open; I turned around again.

The bookburners had begun to sing "What a Friend We Have in Jesus." The words rang through the night in tones piercing and clear, everyone believing in the lyrics, selling the song, and continuing to look at the fire through those small-animal eyes. Humane Inquisitors, they were—scarring no flesh, drawing no blood, breaking no bones; their crimes were against reasonable judgment, not humanity. Yet the sky seemed to darken a little as the music began, the eventual dawn to slip a few minutes further away.

What a friend we have in Jesus,
All our sins and griefs to bear.
What a privilege to carry
Everything to God in prayer.

The concert lasted almost an hour, hymn after hymn after hymn, voices growing stronger as the night wore on and the fire kept snapping, as if through volume alone could the singers convince themselves of the justice of literature made ash.

The first song I heard was the only one I recognized. There was nothing on the bill from Woody Guthrie.

Several books by Mark Twain were extinguished on that forlorn occasion: *The Prince and the Pauper, A Connecticut Yankee in King Arthur's Court, Adventures of Tom Sawyer,* and of course that old standby at uprisings against the excesses of the printed word, *The Adventures of Huckleberry Finn.* At least three copies of the latter went up in smoke, one so old it may have been valuable.

The author would not have been surprised. He might even have expressed satisfaction. The first people who objected to his story of Huck and Jim and their life on the Mississippi were the officials of a library in a small but historic Massachusetts town, who found the book "trash and suitable only for the slums."

"Those idiots in Concord are not a court of last resort," Twain fumed when he learned of the controversy, "and I am not disturbed by their moral gymnastics. No other book of mine has sold so many copies within 2 months after issue as this one. . . . They have given us a rattling tip-top puff which will go into every paper in the country. . . . That will sell 25,000 copies for us sure."

He was wrong. Within two months of the prediction, *The Adventures of Huckleberry Finn* had sold fifty thousand copies. It has not stopped selling since. Twain had underestimated the number, but knew full well the paradox that is censorship's very core.

In colonial times, it was the custom to ring bells and fire cannon to announce public celebrations. To those who voted for him, Thomas Jefferson provided a reason for such festivity by being elected the third president of the United States in 1800. To those who preferred the incumbent John Adams, the election was the end of the Federalist dream. Jefferson and Aaron Burr each received seventy-three electoral votes, Adams sixty-five; Jefferson was awarded the presidency by the House of Representatives.

The night before the new president was to be inaugurated, a man who had cast his ballot for Adams, "an aristocrat," decided to make his frustration known. He stole the clapper from the bell in his local church so that triumphant Jeffersonians would not have the pleasure of hearing it clang the next morning. "A protesting witness saw a lesson" in the theft, writes Dumas Malone in the fourth of his six volumes on Jefferson's life. The witness knew that the newspapers would report the incident, and thus commented to a friend "that the man who removed the clapper was defeating his own ends, for now the bell would be heard all over the continent, instead of merely in that one single town."

And so it was. So it still is when a clapper is secreted away, or an attempt made to do so. Readers, after all, are by definition a curious lot. We are sure to start at the sound of a silent bell. In all likelihood, we will find something irresistible in its melody.

PART TWO

PRESENT

Illustration from an article about Giotto di Bondone, in John Forbes-Robertson, *The Great Painters of Christendom* (New York: Cassell & Co., 1877), p. 26.

Deciding What to Believe

The question did not occur to me in the early days. Not when I was reading Sir James M. Barrie, not when I was pretending to play ball with Chip Hilton and his pals or solve mysteries with the Hardy Boys. It might have crossed my mind in high school, when I was introduced to Shakespeare, reading the bowdlerized versions so as not to have my sensibilities jolted, or it might have struck me in college, when I took up Stendhal and de Maupassant, Bernard Shaw and C. S. Lewis, and first became aware of the remarkable variety of literary styles and themes that awaited my attention. Then again, the question might not have arisen until many years later, when, wanting to produce a book of my own, I could glimpse the impossibility of a single answer.

Why does a writer write?

If his thoughts can be censored and his character maligned, his body wracked by Inquisitors and his freedom denied by tyrants, what is the point of putting pen to paper, fingers to keyboard?

If Protagoras can be exiled and Galileo imprisoned, Mark Twain branded a racist and Frank Baum an advocate of witchcraft; if Jonathan Swift can be taken literally and James Baldwin not taken at all, Stephen Crane castigated for refusing to equate guts with glory and Anne Frank reviled for insufficient chirpiness in the face of holocaust; if Salman Rushdie can be driven into lonely,

101

haunted exile, with sightings of him less frequent than those of the post-mortal Elvis Presley, and his life as a public figure effectively destroyed—if all of this has happened in the past and repetitions ever threaten, what reason could there be for a writer to bare his soul and invite readers to cast their eyes toward him?

If the Christians can attack him for heresy and the heretics for orthodoxy; if he is too liberal for the conservatives and too conservative for the liberals, too optimistic for the pessimists, too forthcoming for the reticent, too passionate for the indifferent, too gritty for the genteel, too whimsical for the earnest, too worldly for the provincial, too spiritual for the bottom-lined, too erudite for the simple-minded, and too long-winded for those who find a sound bite a suitable forum for the explication of political controversy and a highlight package an ample substitute for the five balletic sets of a Wimbledon final, what is the incentive for a writer to return to his desk morning after morning?

If an entire day's output can be a paragraph that is retouched the next day, and an entire month's output a chapter that is lopped off the final draft, and an entire year's output a volume that makes so rapid a transit from printing press to second-hand store that its moments in L.A.'s Book Soup or Washington, D.C.'s Politics and Prose or Westport, Connecticut's Klein's seem but a misstep; if backache and eyestrain are constant afflictions, and self-doubt so much a part of the air he breathes that Van Wyck Brooks began each day "with the same odd feeling, that I am on trial for my life and will probably not be acquitted," and John Steinbeck confessed the main thing for him at times was "to get as many words on paper as possible and then to destroy the paper"; if the consolations of co-workers are denied to the writer by the nature of her work, and those of booze because of its counterproductivity, how does she explain to herself what she does for a living?

Her agent doesn't understand her and her editor is never in and the man who does the art for her dust jackets, not realizing that *of course* you can judge a book by its cover, that's the whole *point* of a cover, to help a reader *judge* a book—have you ever seen a blood-stained corpse or a policeman's badge or a smoking gun on the jacket of a book that's *not* about crime, or a swooning damsel in the arms of a leering hunk on a book that's *not* a romance?— the damned guy who does the art for the covers of her book hasn't come up with an eye-catching design since Thomas Costain last showed up on the bestseller lists.

And her publicist doesn't pay enough attention to her and the sales force is always pushing somebody else's book and the pasty-faced teenagers with retro hairdos and rings in their noses who work at the chain stores in strip malls hardly ever give her a decent position on the shelves, and when they do they turn her book spine out instead of cover out, so that a browser's eyes flit right by it, assuming it is not worthy of full display, something there just to bookend the really commercial stuff.

It is not an unreasonable question. A buyer has a legitimate interest in a seller's motives, a pupil in those of a teacher. A reader wants to know why a writer writes.

If the plan is to get rich, he is fooling himself. True, he no longer needs to dedicate his books to wealthy noblemen; for the past three or four centuries he has been able to earn a few bucks from sales to the public. But only a few. Most writers live at sub-sistence levels: drive used Yugos without cellular phones, live in suburbs without cachet, and wear polo shirts without horse insignias and athletic shoes endorsed by guys who have since been cut from their teams and then nabbed by undercover cops in drug busts outside transvestite bars. They clip coupons, buy generic brands, plan their vacations around airline fare wars and off-season rates at resorts where the principal attraction is a minia-ture golf course in the lobby. They ogle the babes on the beach, but marry the women with full-time jobs and health insurance for the entire family.

Their houses and their self-respect are rented, and it is a struggle each month to come up with the proper payments. Their pride is as scuffed as their shoes, and their horizons so limited that they believe they are earning the undying gratitude of their children by springing for a happy meal once a month at McDonald's. Any more often than that, they explain, and the kids will keep getting the same toy.

"Wouldn't want that, now would we?"

In unison: "No, Daddy."

Maybe a writer can finagle a $30,000 advance for a book, but it will take him so long to write that his hourly rate works out to about the same as the guys who stuff the rodent remains into all-beef hot dogs. Maybe a magazine will pay him $2,000 for an article, but by the time the check is in the mail, he is $3,000 overdrawn at the bank and too depressed to start on his next piece. Maybe a women's club will cough up $500 for a luncheon speech, but the chicken will be tough and the vegetables limp and in the question-and-answer period the ladies will find out that he and John Irving got drunk together one night after a seminar they were conducting on the future of the novel in the post-literate society and will hound him unmercifully for insights on Garp.

If the plan is to be famous, a writer is fooling himself even more. In the age of PC, VCR, VDT, MTV, HSN, and on the verge of HDTV, DAT, and who knows what other sets of initials that portend technology's continuing boom and literacy's unending bust, a writer is more likely to be perceived as quaint than renowned, as much in step with the needs and values of late twentieth-century America as a blacksmith or a corporate ethicist. Maybe he gets three minutes to plug his book on "Good Morning America," but not until a sitcom actress gets six to demonstrate the latest advance in thigh-firmers. Maybe he gets a whole hour on "Donahue," but only as part of a panel that includes three hookers, two diet doctors, and a pederast-turned-Sudanese missionary. Maybe *People* magazine gives his book a two-paragraph review, but he gave the book 420 pages.

If the writer wants the respect of his peers, the odds are slim. Henry James found George Eliot's *Middlemarch* "an indifferent whole." Thomas Carlyle charged Ralph Waldo Emerson with being a "hoary-headed and toothless baboon." Emerson, in turn, was "at a loss" to understand the popularity of Jane Austen, her novels seeming to him "vulgar in tone, sterile in artistic invention, imprisoned in the wretched conventions of English society, without genius, wit or knowledge of the world." Of James Fenimore Cooper's most famous effort, an unimpressed Mark Twain said, "In one place in Deerslayer, and in the restricted space of two-thirds of a page, Cooper has scored 114 offences against literary art out of a possible 115. It breaks the record." And long before any of this modern mud-slinging, Aristophanes dismissed Euripides as a "cliché anthologist . . . and maker of ragamuffin manikins."

If a writer wants the respect of critics, his odds are even slimmer. *The Saturday Review* called *The Great Gatsby* "an absurd story." *The Weekly Review* accused *Main Street* of being "a bulky collection of scenes, types, caricatures, humorous episodes and facetious turns of phrase." The *North British Review* opined that, in Emily Brontë's *Wuthering Heights,* "all the faults of *Jane Eyre* (by Charlotte Brontë) are magnified a thousand fold, and the only consolation which we have in reflecting upon it is that it will never be generally read." And *Century* magazine declared that *A Tale of Two Cities* was "so insincere, such a transparent make-believe, a mere piece of acting."

If a writer wants the respect of the general populace, his odds are slimmest of all. Most people never heard of him. A few, unfortunately, have. In *Bare Bones: Conversations on Terror with Stephen King,* the author tells of the first time he saw someone reading a book of his in public. The book was *Carrie.* King was thrilled. He screwed up his courage, walked over to the person, and asked her how she liked his work. "I think it's *shitty,*" came the response. King decided not to offer to inscribe the book. And poor Theodore Geisel, aka Dr. Seuss, who never scared a soul in his life with one of his joyfully rambunctious children's tales, once got a letter from a man on death row. "If your stuff is the kind of stuff they're publishing nowadays," the prisoner wrote not long before his scheduled execution, "I don't so much mind leaving."

So why does a writer write?

His wife doesn't know how he stands it at home all day and his kids wish he had an office in the city like the other kids' dads and the other kids' dads have a multitude of theories to account for his presence in the neighborhood from morning until night, most of them involving a war wound in a part of the anatomy that affects conventional displays of manhood. The neighborhood dads look down on him for his commute, which is all of eight seconds from bedroom to attic library, as well as for his workday wardrobe, which eschews coat and tie in favor of faded jeans, an elbow-holed sweater and a pair of Rockport loafers that have more paint stains on them than a dropcloth. His creditors, horrified by the irregularity of his paychecks, dun him for extra money and additional references up front, and demand more co-signers for a modest loan than appear on petitions in Texas to increase the oil depletion allowance.

To bricklayers he is effete, to cab drivers incomprehensible, to insurance agents impractical, to stockbrokers unworldly, to hail-fellows-well-met misanthropic.

*   *   *

Perhaps a writer writes because of a glitch in the evolutionary process, a rogue gene, which means she could as easily have turned out a concert pianist, a skydiver, or an albino. Otherwise, how do we explain her persistence in the face of penury, her fanaticism in the face of indifference? How do we explain Anthony Trollope, whose novels and tales fill more than fifty volumes, despite the fact that he could write for only three hours a morning before reporting to his full-time job at the post office? How do we explain the Marquis de Sade, whose biographer, Maurice Lever, tells us that during a twelve-year period of incarceration for various perversities in sexual congress, Sade wrote "constantly: novels, novellas, stories, essays, anecdotes, travelogues, historical fragments, literary and philosophical treatises . . . some twenty plays, and nearly two hundred letters"?

And, most incredibly, how do we explain a man whose path may have crossed that of Sade's behind bars, the extraordinary Danry, a Frenchman who preferred that history remember him as M. Latude?

In the middle of the eighteenth century, Latude was not a writer at all, but a soldier down on his luck after the War of Austrian Succession, casting about for a means of earning a living. "Like countless other petty adventurers," writes Simon Schama in *Citizens,* a history of the French Revolution, Latude

> attempted to use the machinery of court favoritism to advance himself but he did so with an unconventionally risky stratagem. In 1750 he wrote a personal letter to Mme Pompadour—alerting her to a letter bomb that would shortly be sent her way. Danry/Latude could be confident of this because he himself was the author of just such a letter. The half-baked plan was very quickly unraveled, and instead of receiving a pension in gratitude for saving the life of the King's Mistress, Latude found himself in the Bastille.

There he promptly embarked on what proved to be his true calling in life: jailbird. He spent almost all of the next quarter-century in one institution or another, mostly the Bastille, mostly as the result of get-rich-quick schemes no better conceived than the bomb alert. He broke out a few times, was caught a few times, and finally, as Schama relates, was returned to prison and deposited "in one of the appalling underground *cachots* to make escape quite impossible."

Latude's only companions were rats, of which, as the months wore on, he grew oddly fond. He "trained them to eat off his plate and to allow him to scratch them around the neck and chin. . . . The scene of an idyll in hell was completed when Latude managed to make a primitive flute out of bits of his iron grille so that, from time to time, he could serenade his rodent friends with an air or a gavotte as they gnawed contentedly on his leavings."

It was while sharing his *cachot* with the rats that Latude made his turn to literature, deciding on a "project reforming the halberdiers and pikemen in the French army, which he was sure the minister of War would want to see." He had no paper? No matter. He "used tablets of bread moistened with saliva and then dried." He had no ink? No problem. He resorted to "his own blood diluted with water." He had no luck? None whatsoever. It is unlikely that word of Latude's efforts ever reached the minister, certain that his manuscript never did, and a fact that the halberdiers and pikemen carried on as they always had.

In 1777, the prisoner was set free. Still under the spell of literature's unpromising muse, he published a book called *Memoirs of Vengeance*. The prose was almost as explosive as the device intended for the royal paramour. Latude lambasted his jailers, execrated the government, decried the state of the entire French society and its prospects for survival. He was cynical, bitter, outraged; sparks flew from his pen like the discharge of firearms. In a matter of days he was making music for the rats again.

Why did M. Latude keep on?

Perhaps he saw writing as one of his few vocational opportunities in life. In a simpler time, it was. As a child, Nathaniel Hawthorne sent a letter to his mother in which he ran through the possibilities as he saw them. "I do not want to be a doctor and live by men's diseases, nor a minister to live by their sins, nor a lawyer and live by their quarrels. So I don't see there is anything left for me but to be an author."

Perhaps, having made a mess of his earthly existence, Latude longed for immortality. The strangers of the future may have seemed more likely to appreciate him than acquaintances of his own time, and the life described on paper may have appeared more meritorious than the one actually lived. Richard Schickel has said that a writer writes in "an attempt to erect a pathetic paper bulwark against death." But is it really so pathetic? There are words on that paper, after all, and it was words that troubled Solon, inflamed Plato, and terrified the Medici family's librarian; words that acted like tremors along the fault lines of society, rattling the foundations of so many churches and states of past and present. More commonly, it is words that educate and enlighten, enrich and inform, bring on laughter and tears and tantalizing bursts of comprehension. With enough words there is a paragraph, with enough paragraphs a story, with enough stories a world that can brim with life and edification, with hopeful prospects and joy.

But the legacy of words is more than vigorous; it is enduring. When a musician dies, we say that he played. When an athlete dies, we say that he ran or jumped or threw. But when an author dies, his work is often cited in the present tense. Thucydides implies and Socrates warns and Durant tells us. As the poet Milton says in the perpetual present in *Areopagitica,* an author's words "contain a potency of life in them"; they can be "as active as that soul was whose progeny they are." It is not immortality of the flesh-and-blood self, of course, but immortality no less than that which is ensured by flesh-and-blood offspring.

Or it may simply be that M. Latude is too singular a case to deserve further consideration. Would Rush Limbaugh have continued to labor over *The Way Things Ought to Be* if it had landed him in a rat-infested, underground prison? Would Jackie Collins have pressed ahead with *Hollywood Kids* if she had had to write it on a piece of old bread, even that marvelous sourdough from the La Brea Bakery? Would Robert James Waller have bequeathed to posterity the slobbering mawkishness of *The Bridges of Madison County* if he had had to render it in his own blood?

None of them would have needed to bother on my account.

But there may be another explanation for M. Latude's perseverance, one whose simplicity is deceptive. Latude may have burned with the passion to express himself. It may have been an insatiable appetite in him, an unquenchable thirst. Latude may have known the boundless energy of ideas, their heave and swell, and may have realized that it is a kind of energy virtually unknown to all but those who possess it. Yet in those individuals it is one of life's most vital forces, primal and overwhelming; it bubbles, churns, constantly surging in the direction of an outlet. The energy of ideas fuels the writer, invigorates him, allays his fear of dying too soon, which is to say, his fear of failing to erect the paper bulwark in time, leaving something important unsaid. Denied an outlet, the energy will eventually boil over, raining down debris on the psyche and leaving the person who has expressed himself incompletely feeling that, as a result, he has lived incompletely as well.

Benjamin Franklin sensed the energy at an early age. His formal schooling consisted of only two years, ending when he was ten so that he could work in his father's soap and candle shop in Boston, where his duties were not so much unrewarding as inappropriate. Franklin was "forever slipping away," writes Catherine Drinker Bowen in *The Most Dangerous Man in America,* "down to the docks or out to the salt marshes for fishing or trapping."

But mostly he daydreamed, heeding the call of inner voices, sometimes talking back to them. For there were great questions in the air when Franklin was coming of age, and the apprentice chandler wanted a chance to answer. What should the relationship be between Crown and colonies, allegiance and independence, taxation and representation? What of the relationship between God and man, man and woman, owner and slave? Will science make the future a new world, unrecognizable from the old? Will art illuminate truths never before suspected? At one time or another, Franklin turned his thoughts to each of these matters, arriving at conclusions on most, opening himself to the rolling thunder of ideas. But it was not enough. A committed reader, Franklin determined to write the words that others would consider, to pass the energy along, much as the wire from his kite would one day be a conduit for electricity, making a spark in the key at the bottom.

Still in his teens, Franklin came across Joseph Addison's essays in *The Spectator,* and found them a revelation. "I had never before seen any of them," he later wrote. "I bought it, read it over and over, and was much delighted with it. I thought the Writing excellent, & wish'd if possible to imitate it."

The Spectator became Franklin's textbook for home study. He pored over its pages to find wisdom available to him nowhere else, and a literary style that beckoned like a siren's song. Catherine Drinker Bowen tells us that he "reproduced pages from memory, or turned them into verse and back again to prose. He made notes of what he read, jumbled the notes like a pack of cards, and after some weeks reduced them to the best order he could before forming full sentences and completing the paper—anything to gain flexibility and enlarge his vocabulary. It was laborious work."

But fruitful. In his autobiography, when not giving evidence of latent Hinduism, Franklin says that, "By comparing my work afterwards with the original, I discovered many faults and amended them; but I sometimes had the Pleasure of Fancying that in certain Particulars of small import, I had been lucky enough to improve the Method of the Language and this encouraged me to think I might possibly in time come be a tolerable English Writer, of which I was extreamly ambitious."

No less so was Thomas Hardy. In his mid- to late twenties, more than a decade before producing such masterpieces as *The Mayor of Casterbridge, Tess of the D'Urbervilles,* and *Jude the Obscure,* Hardy kept a notebook in which he put himself through the most rigorous of drills. He improved his vocabulary by compiling lists of synonyms, and stretched his imagination by making up words of his own—inventing meaning, playing with sound. Over and over, says biographer Michael Millgate, Hardy relied on the Old Testament and *The Book of Common Prayer,* "picking up particular words and using them in modified grammatical form and totally different contexts . . . generating expressive new phrases from the impulses of great models from the past." What he wanted to do, Millgate declares, was learn "ways upon which particular literary effects might best be achieved, a distinctive voice enunciated."

An excerpt from the Hardy notebook follows. What matters is not how comprehensible it is to us, but how important to him, how revealing of the writer's discipline.

Lyrical Meth Find a situn from expce. Turn to Lycs for a form of expressn that has been used for quite a difft situn. Use it. (Same situn from experience may be sung in sev forms.)

Like Franklin before him, Hardy reminds us of an athlete who takes his training seriously, breaking down the larger skills of his game into their most minute parts and practicing each separately. Think of a basketball player. Dribble, stop, set feet. Square shoulders to basket, raise ball over head. Bend elbows, flick wrist, release ball. Follow through with wrist. Follow through with arm.

Swish.

For the author, it is: Find situation, consider words to express it. Choose best of them, arrange in head, refine in head. Commit to paper. Arrange and refine and commit again. Read aloud to test rhythms.

Publish.

Does a writer write to explain her times? No, that is the journalist, trapped in the swamp of daily occurrence, recording only the most obvious impressions, the most immediate sensations. The writer, more often than not, is a person at odds with her times; what she wants to explain is herself.

Does a writer write because, in an age of ephemera, she feels a responsibility toward what is lasting?

Does she write because, in an age of images, she feels a responsibility toward the linear progression of thought?

Does she write because she venerates depth in a time of shallowness, texture in a time of smooth surfaces, reticence in a time of excess?

Does a writer write because, in an age of lies, she is pledging service to the truth? No, that is the journalist again, believing that what is reported accurately is for that reason of value, and that what is reported quickly is therefore of greater service to the reader or viewer than that which is explored with deliberation. The writer has something at once more elaborate and personal in mind than truth in its narrowly literal guise, deeper currents in which to swim. Alexis de Tocqueville spoke in the mid-nineteenth century of the poet, but what he said applies to all who write outside the narrow bounds of journalism. Tocqueville described the poet as one

> who, by expressing a part of what exists, by adding some imaginary touches to the picture, and by combining certain real circumstances, but which do not in fact concurrently happen, completes and extends the work of nature. Thus the object of poetry is not to represent what is true, but to adorn it, and to present to the mind some loftier imagery.

Tocqueville is talking about power, avoiding the word but providing a definition that is almost flawless in its particulars. To add imaginary touches, to combine circumstances, to adorn the truth, which is often so plainly garbed that it passes unnoticed—this is to exercise a degree of control over the details of life that is possible only in the telling, not in the living.

The writer, then, is a benign dictator. A sufferable megalomaniac. Hungry for dominion, but unwilling to oppress the masses, she contents herself with the arrangement of perception. It is enough for her to shift some angles, adjust the volume, extend the shadows of the past over the fields of here and now.

It is enough for her to raise possibilities.

But how do possibilities come into being? What is it that makes a possibility bloom? To say that the writer is as dedicated as Latude is to address the issue of motivation; to say that he is as studious as Franklin or Hardy is to address the issue of preparation. What about procedure? What are the writer's materials and methods? When he sits at the typewriter or word processor, what happens in his brain, and how does that relate to what happens on the page? How does a single thought become a point of view, a personality trait a fully drawn character, a snippet of physical description an easily visualized locale? Are plots worked out meticulously in advance, as if they were algebra problems with multiple unknowns? Or does a writer just start writing, figuring out his destination as he goes along? "Think of it like driving a car at night," says E. L. Doctorow, author of *Ragtime* and *Billy Bathgate*. "You turn on the ignition and put it in drive. You can't see very far ahead, but as long as you keep moving, so does the beam of the headlights in front of you. You're doing forty miles an hour. So is the beam, but it always stays ahead of you eighty or ninety feet. Eventually, the lights will shine on the journey's end, and you'll pull in right behind them."

Does the writer have secrets? Is he willing to reveal them? Is he able? Perhaps, despite the fact that finding words is what he does for a living, he cannot find words to describe the process of finding words, and is left, when questioned, with no choice but to be evasive.

It is not a problem for others. Ask a physicist how he makes measurements on a crystal, and he will tell you that he evaporates electrodes onto the crystal, then attaches an impedance bridge so that the ratio of force per unit to the volume displacement of the surface may be readily determined. Ask a lobbyist how he corrupts a politician and he will tell you a different tale of evaporation and measurement: the wining and dining of the politician until his resistance evaporates, and then, the measure of his susceptibility having thus been taken, the attachment of the quid pro quo, the lobbyist telling the officeholder that his vote has now been purchased, but vowing to him that its sale will, in the long run, benefit the body politic no less than the narrow private interest.

But ask a writer how he writes and his answer will almost surely disappoint. Maybe it will be whimsical: Ring Lardner insisting that he dropped a few widely separated words onto a sheet of paper and then went back later to fill in the spaces. Maybe it will be facetious: Oscar Wilde claiming that he spent the entire morning putting in a comma, the entire afternoon taking it out. Or maybe the writer will be candid, admitting that there is little he can do until inspired, then confessing the lengths to which he goes to court inspiration, some of them nearly inconceivable to those of more rational vocation.

Take Dame Edith Sitwell. She did a great imitation of a corpse. Actually climbed into a coffin, closed her eyes, and folded her arms over her bosom. Threw a switch in her brain, blew out her intellectual circuitry. Imagined the unending void, felt its despair or perhaps its reassurance, wallowed in it for a while—and then snapped to, bolting from the box and heading for her desk and applying pen to paper in a fury of purposefulness, as if she had just entered the room from a more conventional resting place, having completed a less morbidly situated period of preparation. In *A Natural History of the Senses,* Diane Ackerman relates her confusion. "What was it about that dim, constrained solitude that spurred her creativity?" Ackerman asks. "Was it the idea of the coffin or the feel, smell, foul air of it that made creativity possible?"

The French novelist Colette found herself unable to write until she had picked up her cat and plucked off its fleas. One here, one there, soon a dozen, maybe a hundred or more before the first word of the day found its way to the page. Meanwhile there's this pulsating mound of disenfranchised little insects on the floor, wondering what happened to all the damn cat hair. But in Colette's case, Ackerman thinks she understands. The woman was a voluptuary, Ackerman reminds us, and therefore "it's not hard to imagine how the methodical stroking and probing into fur might have focused" her critical faculties.

Katherine Mansfield, who wrote *Ship of Fools,* also needed

focusing, although she preferred flora to fauna as an agent. Mansfield would work among her carnations and begonias before settling in to write; she loved the sight of things growing, the feel of damp earth under her fingernails, and gentle blooms, freshly picked, in her hand. It took "terrific hard gardening," she once said, to transport herself to just the right place in her mind, a place whence the stories would flow.

For Henrik Ibsen, on one occasion at least, what it took was a display of nature's violence. "I had on a table a scorpion in an empty beer glass," he later wrote about his work on a particular play. "From time to time the brute would ail. Then I would throw a piece of ripe fruit into it, on which it would cast itself in a rage and inject its poison into it. Then it was well again." The scorpion kept assaulting the fruit, Ibsen kept watching and writing; thus was the proper ambience fashioned for *Brand,* not one of the author's better-known dramas, but one in which, according to biographer Hans Heiberg, Ibsen "flays both himself and his people, emphasizing that he has lost his trust in both their future and their past."

Historian Jules Michelet, a contemporary of the estimable Latude, chose for a topic the corrupt state of pre-revolutionary France. He sought to woo the muse in a manner even more vile than Ibsen's. Each morning, he would repair to a public urinal and spend half an hour or more sniffing around as avidly as Mansfield in her garden, except that what Michelet inhaled was not the subtle cologne of nature's blossoms, but the acrid, ammoniated fumes of liquid human waste. He breathed in deeply, almost making a study of the bouquet, noting the taste of the scent as it worked his way inside him. "Having come as close as I could to the subject of my horror," Michelet explained about his odd behavior, he was ready to write about a putrescent society.

Similarly, Johann von Schiller kept a supply of rotten apples

117

in his desk. Finding himself at an impasse in his labors, he would lift the top, fill his nasal passages with the odor of the decomposed fruit, and then conjure up just the right word or phrase, something as pungent as it was suitable.

William Faulkner removed the doorknob from his study to keep out visitors; Harold Robbins withdrew the electric ladder to his loft, although, to the regret of millions, he was always able to get it back down again. Also going to extremes in pursuit of solitude was John Steinbeck, who drove his station wagon to a different location every day, having built in it "a work table that sits on the front seat . . . and makes the second seat a work room. It is very comfortable and it will even hold a typewriter. So the first thing every morning I will drive out and park someplace and not come back until I've done my daily stint. It will not only save me from the kids but will save me from myself and all the things I think of that I should be doing when I should be working."

Judith Krantz re-reads the works of Edith Wharton before starting on one of her own volumes, immersing herself in *The Age of Innocence* and then churning out *Princess Daisy*, luxuriating in *The House of Mirth* and slapping together *Mistral's Daughter*, something of frightful import being lost in the translation. Benjamin Franklin and Victor Hugo sometimes disrobed before writing, and T. E. Lawrence went further. Diane Ackerman writes that Lawrence not only shed his clothes, but would occasionally "climb naked up mulberry trees—a fetish of long limbs and rough bark that stimulated his thoughts."

And then there is T. S. Eliot, troubadour of modern angst, manufacturer of ingenious poetic forms to express it. Believing that he did his best work when he had a cold, Eliot would sometimes save an especially difficult passage for a time when so afflicted, perhaps even attempting once or twice to bring on the affliction. "The rustling of his head," says Ackerman, who has obviously made quite a study of such matters, "as if full of petti-coats, shattered the usually logical links between things and allowed his mind to roam."

But then what happens? Eliot is so congested that a whole carton of cold capsules wouldn't help and Sitwell crawls energetically out of her coffin, another resurrection; Lawrence scampers down the tree and gets dressed and Colette's cat is so clean it might have been treated with chemicals. The muse, in other words, has been summoned, and now takes up position at the writer's side, beam-ing at her, whispering encouragement. What does she do next? The juices might be flowing, but how does the tale get told?

Let us ask Faulkner. William Faulkner with his door knob off. William Faulkner bending over the page in the act of creation, maybe somewhere in the early going of *As I Lay Dying*:

> Overhead the day drives level and gray, hiding the sun by a flight of gray spears. In the rain the mules smoke a little, splashed yellow with mud, the off one clinging in sliding lunges to the side of the road above the ditch. The tilted lumber gleams dull yellow, water-soaked and heavy as lead, tilted at a steep angle into the ditch above the broken wheel; about the shattered spokes and about Jewel's ankles a runnel of yellow neither water nor earth swirls, curving with the yellow road neither of earth nor water, down the hill dissolving into a streaming mass of dark green neither of earth nor sky.

How, then, does the story unfold in this way? These words at this moment in the process of structuring thought and rendering it artistically? These images, these rhythms, this mood?

"It's difficult to say just what part of any story comes specif-ically from imagination, what part from experience, what part from observation," Faulkner tried to explain on one occasion. "It's like having . . . three tanks with a collector valve. And you don't know just how much comes from which tank. All you know is a stream of water runs from the valves when you open them from the three tanks—observation, experience, imagination."

All right. First tank, experience, the indispensable starting point. If the reader is to live vicariously through the book, the author must have lived abundantly before writing it. He must have scaled summits and sunk into abysses, completed marathons and stumbled at starting lines, mingled with the throngs and dwelt in utter isolation. He must have laughed and cried, bellowed and whimpered, censured and praised. He must have been sinner and saint, knave and hero and clown. This is not to say that his experiences should have been unique; rather, they should have ranged far in the realm of the typical. He must see clearly, but have had moments of blindness; hear acutely, but have gone through periods of intense silence, what the works of Buddha refer to as "the unbearable repartee." It is the quiet times in which a writer writes, but without tumult there is nothing to say.

He must be indiscriminate, willing to do almost anything for experience; he must be selective, unwilling to repeat himself for the sake of ease or compromise himself for the sake of novelty. He may study English at a university if he chooses, but Dr. Seuss, as quoted by biographers Judith and Neil Morgan, was dubious. "English and writing was my major, but I think that's a mistake. That's teaching you the mechanics of getting water out of a well that may not exist." The writer may take a creative expression class in night school, or find a book on literary technique at the library and study it alone on weekends. But several decades ago, when a young man asked Sinclair Lewis how he should prepare himself for a life in letters, Lewis said, "Run a filling station," and that may still be as good a course as any.

The writer, though, cannot rely solely on his own experience, as it makes up too limited a domain. He is but one person, and humanity a multitude of shared traits, conflicting values and radically differing perspectives. The writer needs a broader vantage point than his own resources can provide, one that embraces people and places and practices which would otherwise be alien to him. Commenting on the work of Leonardo da Vinci, Will Durant writes, "Since any man's experience can be no more than a microscopic fragment of reality, Leonardo supplemented his with reading, which can be experience by proxy."

Second tank, observation, not as easy as it sounds. "I became a transcendent eyeball," said Ralph Waldo Emerson one day, deep in the woods, opening himself to nature's bounties and pitfalls. "I am nothing; I see all." But sight is only the beginning. What is seen must be remembered; what is remembered must be analyzed; what is analyzed must be placed into context and then set down on paper with clarity at the minimum, grace if at all possible. Whereas experience, as a participatory matter, often penetrates several layers deep into a writer's consciousness, observation has been known to strike glancing blows and skitter away wasted, one image replacing the next rather than adding to it. A criminologist will tell you. He knows that the reports of forensic scientists, ballistics experts, laboratory technicians, and fingerprint cataloguers are all more reliable forms of evidence in a legal proceeding than eyewitness identification, which is too often undermined by the subject's inattentiveness.

The writer cannot risk a lack of attention. Rather, he must observe to the point of surfeit, for what the physicist makes of his crystals and the lobbyist of his causes, the writer makes of everything he sees and hears and touches and smells and tastes. Everything he knows and guesses and hopes. He cannot lower his guard, cannot turn himself off. He is his own 7-Eleven, on call as observer twenty-four hours a day, 365 days a year, certain that if he relaxes his vigil long enough to blink, the nugget of his next story will flit by, as if it had been trying all along to escape his notice. There are times when the writer must find his surveillance unbearable, times when he must look at the insomniac and long for so restful a state.

Third tank, imagination, the least understood of the ingredients. To the British philosopher Thomas Hobbes, imagination is "decaying sense," a notion that contributes to the belief that the more successful one is as an artist, the less stable he is as a human being, that the tumult out of which a writer writes is a permanent condition, untreatable and in a constant state of metastasis. This is the view of the author as drunk, wife-beater, sexual deviant; as neurotic, psychotic, paranoiac; as rebel, outcast, misfit. You might like to read the guy's books, but you wouldn't want him coaching your little girl's soccer team.

Kenneth Grahame, who wrote *The Wind in the Willows*, believes that imagination is a "higher gift"; poet Wallace Stevens that it is "a force of nature" in "the world of words"; historian Thomas Macaulay that it is "the wings of an ostrich," which enable a person "to run though not to fly." There is in each of these definitions and in many others that could be cited a hint of something mystical, the writer dependent upon external forces, hoping that genius will light from elsewhere, as opposed to its being present within and put to use by the author when needed.

Social critic Malcolm Muggeridge, though, is among those who find the process less supernatural. He says that imagination is "seeing into the *meaning* of things rather than seeing things." A form of observation, then, but at 20/20 and with perfect recall, down to details not retained by most people and not even apparent to the eye. The author, in this scenario, is critic, scholar, soothsayer; the muse is lady-in-waiting.

But however imagination is defined, its importance is irrefutable. It is a transforming medium, a catalyst, a broker without whose services means and ends cannot be united. Through the employment of imagination, a writer converts the raw materials of experience and observation into a finished literary product: a biography that illuminates its subject, a history that illuminates its time, a novel that illuminates the man or woman who wrote it, as well as the world therein created.

Without imagination, a writer is just this person hanging around life with a ball-point pen, taking frantic dictation from events.

Is the writer a storyteller? If so, he judges his work by the speed at which the reader turns his pages. He does not deal in words so much as scenes, and is often so eager to construct the latter that his treatment of the former is awkward, as if he resents the necessity of having to cope with units so small and yet demanding as single, English morphemes. Setting is not important to him; nuance only slows things down; characters are made of cardboard for ease of assembly. It is diversion that this writer means to create, not art or a certain attitude or behavior in the reader—and the storyteller is sometimes bewildered by the fact that even those who enjoy his books do not long remember them or take them seriously.

Is the writer a propagandist? If so, he judges his work by the extent to which the reader is roused to action. Does he accept the author's advice on voting for public officials, eating wisely, losing weight, gaining confidence, dressing successfully, managing time? On eliminating backache, avoiding colds, handling men, handling women, achieving orgasm, withstanding menopause, grooming pets, improving memory? On investing in mutual funds, purchasing real estate, thwarting probate, running a small business, surviving the loss of a loved one, or getting in touch with the child inside? It is an attitude or behavior on the part of the reader that the propagandist means to create, not art or diversion.

Is the writer a stylist? Then he judges his work on more personal grounds, by standards of his own, approaching the language much like a cabinetmaker approaches his supply of wood, wanting merely to make of it the best structure he can, unconcerned with the value that others place on it, or even who the others are. He is enamored of detail, does things over and over and delights in the repetition; he finds as much pleasure in the sanding as in the sale. The most selfish of writers, he believes that the judgments that matter most are his own; the most selfless, he allows the reader to decide for himself what to feel, whether to act. It is art he means to create, not behavior or diversion.

Is the writer an opportunist? Then he has few standards at all, and those are matters of commerce, not literature. He is simply a person who dresses up in author's garb for a time because he wants to capitalize on the fame he has acquired in another field, or because he once worked for someone famous and has dirt to dish, or once had sex with someone famous and can do a play-by-play. It is neither art nor attitude nor diversion he means to create, solely income, and in the aftermath of the greed-besotted, literacy-starved eighties, it is the opportunist-as-author who reigns supreme. His book has been on the *New York Times* bestseller list for half a year; he has made so many appearances on television talk shows that people are beginning to think of him as a cohost; and his fees for a lecture are so high that every time he opens his mouth he adds a car to one of his garages or a garage to one of his homes.

The question that did not occur to me in the early days now comes with increasing frequency, an inner voice grown insistent with the years. I hear it faintly as I read a new suspense novel by Robert Goddard or an old one by Wilkie Collins, hear it as if through a loudspeaker as I begin each day's work on *The Joy of Books.*

Why does a writer write?

Faulkner says, "To help man endure by lifting his heart," but can so blatant an expression of altruism be trusted?

Gore Vidal says, "To set a chime of words tinkling in the minds of fastidious people," but there is too much tinkle in the response.

Poet Stanley Kunitz writes, he claims, "For money, rage and love," but he is too sweeping, his comment not related enough to actual practice of the craft.

George Herbert tells us he writes, "To once more smell the dew and rain," but this is a seventeenth-century English poet speaking. As an answer to a question so vexing as authorial motive, Herbert's words seem too . . . well, poetic.

Erica Jong closes in on at least one truth when she refers to "the ecstasy of watching my scrawl cover the pages. It is the sort of trance saints speak of." Such a potent vanity does Jong confess, but harmless, even refreshing in its lack of guile.

Alfred Kazin approaches another truth when he says, "In a very real sense, the writer writes in order to teach himself, to understand himself, to satisfy himself; the publishing of his ideas, though it brings gratification, is a curious anti-climax." In other words, Kazin believes that books are the fruits of utter self-absorption, eagerly shared.

Still another truth is provided by Graham Greene, who calls writing "the escaper's royal road," a sentiment echoed by a much-acclaimed American playwright, a man whose drunken father called him Miss Nancy, whose mother drifted in and out of reality as if it were an afternoon nap, and whose sister was so violent a schizophrenic that she eventually underwent a frontal lobotomy. My typewriter, said Tennessee Williams, "became my place of retreat, my cave, my refuge."

But historian Max Lerner has no patience with this navel-contemplating, this flowery phrase-making. "You write a book not for the elaborate reasons you spell out," Lerner insists, "but mainly because you can't help it." The explanation is not as superficial as it seems. The causes of any compulsion being largely mysterious, Lerner is probably telling all that his conscious mind knows. In the process of exercising control over the details of life, Lerner realized that he was in the grip of a higher power, and that it was not as important for him to identify that power or elucidate it as it was to accede to its will. Writing was a biological imperative for Lerner, like breathing or eating or sleeping, or as H. L. Mencken would have it, like attaining "that feeling of tension relieved and function achieved which a cow enjoys on giving milk."

Stephen King is of similar mind, but if Mencken feels the release of pressure, King feels it building up, as Sheriff Pangborn felt his dread growing with increasing awareness of Leland Gaunt's real business in *Needful Things*. You don't write for money, King says, "or you're a monkey. You don't think of the bottom line, or you're a monkey. You don't think of it in terms of hourly wage, yearly wage, even lifetime wage, or you're a monkey. In the end, you don't even do it for love, although it would be nice to think so. You do it because to not do it is suicide." Which is, perhaps, the ultimate Stephen King horror story.

As a reader, I want to believe otherwise. I want to believe that a writer writes to celebrate life, not to stave off the impulse to end it abruptly; to make sense of the seeming disorder, not to yield to it in despair. I want to believe that a writer portrays sorrow so hauntingly that the reader may more easily appreciate joy, loss so brutally that the reader may more diligently pursue gain, loneliness so wrenchingly that the reader may more richly prize community. This is not self-delusion; it is, rather, a reader's bill of rights, his own version of adding imaginary touches, combining circumstances, adorning the plain-garbed truth.

And so I choose to think that Charles Dickens was more cheered by the pluck of his underdogs than dismayed by the viciousness of his capitalists, that Sir Arthur Conan Doyle admired Holmes's ingenuity more than he recoiled at Moriarty's deviousness, that Thomas Hardy treasured the small joys of life more than he lamented their frightening brevity.

I choose to think that George Bernard Shaw's verbal pyrotechnics were meant to produce debate, not destruction, and that Jonathan Swift's invective, like so much homeopathic medicine, was ultimately salubrious in effect, not toxic.

I also choose to think that . . .

John Updike sends his sentences gavotting through fiction and essay alike because he rejoices in such old-fashioned displays of grace.

Tom Wolfe cascades his words over the page because he is exuberant at the sight of such torrents, and at the plosive sounds they make as they pop and splash against paper.

Robert B. Parker composes his dialogues between Spenser and Hawk because their rock-and-roll rhythms get his feet tapping and fingers snapping and lips curling up at the corners into the kind of slyly adolescent grin that is otherwise impossible for a grownup to achieve.

Kazuo Ishiguro erects his intricate edifices of doubt and subterfuge because of the pride he feels in making such seemingly fragile structures bear such incredible weight.

Richard Brautigan made up his lunatic lands of causelessness and noneffect so that the places in which he resided in real life would seem sane by comparison.

Part Two: Present

Pete Dexter's barbarities and perversions are indirect acknowledgment of a greater truth, that kindness and normality are more readily encountered in this life.

Richard Schickel's essays on society and cinema are so acerbic in their dislikes because the author is so vulnerable in his passions.

Barbara Tuchman embarked on her random strolls into the past because she knew the byways she had discovered were more profoundly scenic than the main-traveled roads of more conventional historians.

David McCullough, who also renders the past in terms vivid and unforgettable, is as a result a more vigorous participant in the here and now.

Scott Turow depicts the law in a gloomy and labyrinthine manner because, his doubts thus expunged, he is free to stand before the bar with pride in the value of his calling.

And I choose to think that Elmore Leonard delights in his demimondes, Ed McBain in his precinct houses, Michael Crichton and Thomas Gifford in their ever-shifting venues of mechanistic and historical menace, and Thomas H. Cook, the unknown master, in his inspired reworkings of the entire format of mystery fiction, such eerie jangling poetry does he weave through situations no longer tried-and-true.

I choose to think that John Steinbeck was gladdened by the revelries of Cannery Row, Willa Cather sustained by the endless roll of the plains, Nathaniel Hawthorne heartened by the unearthly solitude of a New England wood, John D. MacDonald stimulated by the sweltering intrigues of a Florida summer, and Sir James M. Barrie tickled by the shenanigans of the land he created himself, the one beyond the second star to the right, the place you can get to through the air, but not by plane.

I choose to think that E. L. Doctorow is basically light-hearted and Joseph Wambaugh fundamentally optimistic and even Stephen King, for all the pessimism he professes and the oppression he implies, not to mention the stomach-roiling grotesqueries he splatters across his pages in full color and fuller detail, that even King himself is more often than not kindly disposed toward the everyday world and those who call it home.

These are a few of my favorite authors. They tell me what to read. I decide what to believe. I am, after all, a figure of some standing in the community of books, a completer of literary scenarios. Have been ever since I was a kid.

THE PHILOSOPHER.

"The Philosopher" by Frans Van Mieris (1635–1681), in John Forbes-Robertson, *The Great Painters of Christendom* (New York: Cassell & Co., 1877), p. 224.

$\mathcal{A}$ Place of One's Own

$\mathcal{T}$he serious reader in the age of technology is a rebel by definition: a protester without placard, a Luddite without hammer or bludgeon. She reads on planes to picket the antiseptic nature of modern travel, on commuter trains to insist on individualism in the midst of the herd, in hotel rooms to boycott the circumstances that separate her from her usual sources of comfort and stimulation, during coffee breaks to escape from the banal conversation of office mates, and at home to revolt against the pervasive and mind-deadening irrelevance of television.

She reads in her living room and her kitchen, in her bedroom and her finished basement. In the bathroom, she opens her book on the toilet and in the tub, the latter a practice that dates back at least as far as the eighteenth century, when a man identified by Barbara Tuchman only as "a learned German" had an edition of Homer printed on slabs of rubber, so that it could withstand not only wet hands but an occasional, inadvertent dunking.

The serious reader reads in lines at supermarkets, movie theatres, museums, banks, post offices, airports, amusement parks, zoos, football stadiums, and car washes. She reads in styling salons, doctors' offices, driver's license renewal centers, muffler repair shops, and traffic jams on hopelessly knotted highways. She reads, like Sara Gaskell in Michael Chabon's novel *Wonder Boys,* "standing in front of the microwave with a book in one hand and a fork in the other, heating a cup of noodle soup." She reads at playgrounds while her kids hang from monkey bars, at malls while her spouse shops for clothes, in restaurants before the meal is served, at health clubs as she pedals an exercise bicycle, and at swimming pools between dips. She dives into her books, floats from page to page, comes up for air once every so often but finds life in a submerged state no less salubrious to her nature.

She is like this now. She has always been like this. As a child, H. L. Mencken would sit "on the high marble front steps of our house in Hollins Street, in the quiet of approaching dusk, and hearing my mother's warnings that reading by failing light would ruin my eyes. The neighborhood apprentices to gang life went howling up and down the sidewalk, trying to lure me into their games of follow your-leader and run-sheep-run, but I was not to be lured, for I had discovered . . . a new and powerful enchantment."

On reaching his maturity, Mencken looked back on those days, on the discoveries he made between the covers of his first books, and said that they "give a boy a considerable thrill, and augment his sense of dignity. It is no light matter, at eight, to penetrate suddenly to the difference between *to, two* and *too,* or to that between *run* in baseball and *run* in topographical science, or *cats* and *Katz.* The effect is massive and profound, and at least comparable to that which flows, in later life, out of filling a royal flush or debauching the wife of a major-general of cavalry."

The serious reader's ancestors are many, and even a partial list impresses. Samuel Johnson once became so entranced while poring over a volume that he leaned into the candle on his bedstead, burning his wig. Theodore Roosevelt burned his shoes, so engrossed was he in a book that he did not realize he had put his feet up on the fireplace. Upton Sinclair admitted that he "would be missing at a party and be discovered behind the sofa with a book." Sherwood Anderson said that he "went fishing with a book under my arm, went to ball games and read in a book between innings." And Percy Bysshe Shelley was lucky not to have been trampled by fellow pedestrians or run over by a carriage; an acquaintance tells us that Shelley had "a book in his hand at all hours; reading . . . at table, in bed, and especially during a walk . . . not only at Oxford . . . but in the most crowded thoroughfares of London."

A friend of mine who lives in New York has taken to rating his books on the basis of how many subway stops he misses while absorbed in them. A one-stopper, he says, happens to him every few weeks, a two-stopper a few times a year, and a three-stopper only once in his life. It was, fittingly, Edmund Morris's magnificent biography, *The Rise of Theodore Roosevelt,* and the particular point of immersion was chapter nine, Valentine's Day, 1884, when Roosevelt's mother, Mittie, and his first wife, Alice, died under the same roof within a twelve-hour period. Mittie left him first, at three in the morning, even though in death she "looked as beautiful as ever, with her 'moonlight' complexion and ebony-black hair untouched by gray." Morris says that Roosevelt felt a "bewildering agony of soul" at the moment, and in that wretched state "climbed back upstairs and again took Alice Lee into his arms."

> Day dawned, but the fog outside grew thicker, and gaslight continued to burn in the Roosevelt mansion. About mid-morning, a sudden, violent rainfall miraculously cleared the air, and for five minutes the sun shone on muddy streets and streaming rooftops. The weather seemed about to break, but clouds closed over the city once more. By noon the temperature was 58 degrees, and the humidity grew intolerable. Then, slowly, the fog began to lift, and dry cold air blew in from the northeast.
>
> At two o'clock, Alice died.

133

And Theodore Roosevelt, with so much of his life yet to live and so many of his accomplishments yet to savor, went to his diary, drew a cross under February 14, and wrote: "The light has gone out of my life."

My friend said he was lucky he missed only three stops. The way he felt that day at the bottom of page 241 of Morris's book, he could have ridden his Manhattan subway to another borough and then across the state line into a new time zone. He might have noticed, but he wouldn't have minded.

The uncomprehending sometimes refer to this kind of intense concentration in the reader as absent-mindedness, but the philosopher William James knew that that is just a word meaning "present-mindedness somewhere else."

The serious reader expands his circle of acquaintances, but is not unhappy with his friends.

He expands his knowledge of place, but is not dissatisfied with home.

He expands his awareness of self, but is not confused about his identity, his responsibilities, or his beliefs.

He believes that other media overemphasize the modern, undervalue the traditional, and barely acknowledge the timeless. Seventy-millimeter movies do not fill his field of vision like the scope of great novels; quadraphonic sound does not reverberate within him like the voice of a thoughtful author; and as far as he is concerned, interactive video is just another name for a lucidly reasoned page: black letters bounding off white paper as if magnetically repelled, triggering a response in the reader that clarifies a meaning in the book which, in turn, triggers the next response. And back and forth like that, back and forth, producing, in the words of a reader named Dylan Thomas, "the gusts and grunts and hiccups and hee-haws of the common fun of the earth." As quoted in *The Open Door: When Writers First Learned to Read,* Thomas went on to admit that it was occasionally too much for him; he could hardly keep up with "the shape and shade and size and noise of the words as they hummed, strummed, jigged and galloped along."

But Thomas had to concede that it "was the time of innocence" of which he wrote. He knew that his sentiments had a curiously old-fashioned ring to them in the age of technology.

The serious reader is not engaged by technology. A computer program is an occasional convenience to him, not a talisman for an alternative culture. He takes no pleasure in the heft of a floppy disk, cannot flip the pages of a CD-ROM. He knows that the ROM version of *The Grapes of Wrath* offers a map of the Joad family's route west, but the reader can find maps of his own if so inclined, and they will be larger, able to be touched and folded. He knows that the ROM shows the photographs that inspired Steinbeck to write the book, but the visual quality of photos on a computer screen, with its gray-green humming light, is reminiscent of TV pictures from the early fifties. He knows that the ROM contains interviews with friends of Steinbeck, but does not understand what these have to do with the tale. He wants to read the book, for heaven's sake, not flit around the periphery of it like a manic graduate student with his thesis due. "Somewhere in there lurks the novel's text," wrote Sarah Lyall, reviewing *The Grapes of Wrath: The Rom* for the *New York Times,* "which almost seems beside the point next to the souped-up new features."

The serious reader may be plugged into the Internet, but not for purposes literary. The information superhighway may speed him to certain of his destinations, but a book is a back road, a scenic route along undeveloped acreage and clear-running streams, and he will take it whenever he can.

Part Two: Present

* * *

He agrees with George Bernard Shaw that people need trash on their shelves as well as classics, but finds the latter more true to his nature. Diversion is the occasional need, but knowledge the constant quest.

And the serious reader defines knowledge in his own way. It is not a commodity to him, that which is bartered in the marketplace for an agreed-upon number of dollars per week plus vacation time and fringe benefits. Rather, "Knowledge Its Own End," as a chapter title has it from John Henry Newman's nineteenth-century classic, *The Idea of a University*—meaning that knowledge is something the reader prizes for its own sake, as he would an object that is purely beautiful or a person whose standards are not subject to fluctuation by whim. The reader finds a piquancy to knowledge as it settles into the mind that is comparable to the taste of a delicate food as it slowly melts onto the palate—a hedonistic view of learning to be sure, lush and impractical, but one he shares with countless other men and women over the centuries who, of impractical bent themselves, were nonetheless capable of great worldly achievement. Theodore Roosevelt read a book a day and still led the strenuous life. Bertrand Russell read a book a day and still led the impassioned life. And Don Quixote, who should not be taken lightly either because of his fictional status or his dementia, read so much that his "imagination became filled with a host of fancies," so much "as to lead him almost wholly to forget the life of a hunter and even the administration of his estate"—and he still led the adventurous life.

For Thomas Jefferson, it was an unexpected life; so much happened to him that he had never envisioned, so many honors, so much tribulation. As a boy, though, his days were like those of his friends: he read books, of course; he swam and rode horses, fished and hunted for fowl. Biographer Willard Sterne Randall says that Jefferson and his sister often "wandered in the lowlands and searched for bluebells." If he had dreams of extraordinary missions, they are not recorded.

Yet, among other accomplishments, the adult Jefferson would write the Declaration of Independence, serve two terms as president of the United States, and found the University of Virginia. The first made the colonies a nation; the second made the nation a larger and more philosophically secure place; the third provided all universities to follow with a model of excellence, both academic and architectural.

Still, there were certain needs within Jefferson, as within all serious readers, unmet by accomplishment on so public a scale. What a person does for the world, he wants to do; what he does for himself, he *needs* to do. Perhaps this is self-centeredness, but hardly a virulent strain; only when the inner person is recharged can the outer be a fit companion, or adversary, for the people and events he encounters. "The enormities of the times," Jefferson wrote late in life, had taken him from his library and "the delightful pursuit of knowledge." It was a great regret. Jefferson thought of his books as "mental furniture"; he was never truly comfortable without them.

To John Adams, long after their political enmity had evolved into a warm, mutually bracing friendship, Jefferson admitted what Adams and most of his other companions already knew. "I could not live without my books." He was not complaining; not, as people today might think, lamenting a weakness or an addiction. He was simply stating a fact, a condition of fruitful existence.

A serious reader himself, Adams understood. Many years earlier, in a letter to his wife from England, he complained about the amount of traveling he had done in the service of the new American nation: "This wandering, itinerating Life grows more and more disagreeable to me. I want to see my Wife and Children every Day, I want to see my Grass and Blossoms and Corn, &c. every Day. I want to see my Workmen. . . . But above all except the Wife and Children I want to see my Books."

Most of the volumes for which Adams longed were passed down to his children and grandchildren, and inspired the later generations of his family to write brilliant books of their own in history, travel, and autobiography.

The Jefferson collection was the start of the grandest literary archive in America, the Library of Congress.

The serious reader fears for the state of formal education. Fifteen million adult Americans cannot join her in the pleasures of a book, and another seventy-five million have only "minimal" reading skills. There is, in these recent statistics, an ineffable sadness.

But it is not illiteracy that troubles her so much as aliteracy; not the inability to read, which is often overcome, but the unwillingness, born of indolence, fatigue, or preoccupation. Researchers Lawrence Stedman, Katherine Tinsley, and Carl Kaestle have noted that before the emergence of the electronic age, "book buying spread to a majority of the population, and low-income groups increased their book buying." More recently, though, the amount of money people spend on books has "decreased drastically as a percentage of total, recreational, mass-media and electronic-item spending."

It is all manifest in the schools.

In the past few years, studies have shown that a significant number of American high school students cannot place either the Civil War or World War I in its proper half-century. They have heard of Joseph Stalin and Winston Churchill, but can provide no information about them, not even the nations they once led or the fact that they were indeed leaders of nations. They do not know who wrote *Uncle Tom's Cabin,* cannot name a single contemporary American poet, and believe that the Alamo, if the name rings a bell at all, is an epic poem from ancient Greece. They comprehend what they read below grade level, retain below grade level. They do math below grade level, science below grade level. They even understand the concept of grade level below grade level.

Yet their shortcomings, rather than being a scarlet letter to them, are often a badge. They wear them proudly, like a baseball cap turned backwards; they wear them blatantly, like a pair of pants riding halfway down the hips, cuffs scraping the ground. They are well aware of what society values: unlettered athletes with multimillion-dollar endorsement contracts, and ignorant rock stars whose concerts are standing room only. As a result, the students are as likely to laugh off their vacuity as to be chastened by it or motivated to improve. There is, in fact, the quality of a joke to some of what they don't know.

Even those who subject themselves to the rigors of written language with some frequency are reaping less from it than did previous generations. Retired Cornell professor Donald Hayes teamed up with a computer to sample 788 textbooks in use between 1860 and 1920, and compared them to today's books, finding that, "Honors high school texts are no more difficult than an eighth grade reader was before World War II." This is the so-called dumbing down of America, lower expectations meant to give the illusion of improved performance. To many people, it seems a benevolent impulse, a natural outgrowth of egalitarian principles. In reality, it is proof that the kinds of information once considered a necessity for high school students have become a luxury, possessed by only a few and no longer widely appreciated.

Other studies show that college students are also becoming strangers to the printed page. Too many cannot distinguish between the ideas contained in the Constitution and those espoused by Karl Marx, do not know what the Magna Carta is, draw a blank when it comes to Reconstruction. They cannot name even one of the Great Lakes, and are unable to place the former Soviet Union on a map. When asked who wrote *The Tempest, Crime and Punishment,* or *Pride and Prejudice,* their eyes flicker but their brains do not engage. Some have heard of the volumes, some know the authors, but few can match one group to the other.

It is as true of students at prestigious schools as it is of those at more middling institutions. In 1992, twelve undergraduates at the University of Pennsylvania, under the baton of adjunct associate professor Frank Luntz, surveyed more than three thousand of their fellow Ivy Leaguers, and, among other things, found that half of them did not know the senators from their home states. More than a third could not name the prime minister of Britain, and three-quarters had no idea who was responsible for the phrase, "government of the people, by the people, and for the people." Another quarter could not give the number of justices on the United States Supreme Court.

A few years earlier, education critic Diane Ravitch uncovered her own tale of horror from the Ivy League. "Typical is the story of the Harvard *senior,*" she wrote in the *New York Times,* compelled to italicize the young man's school year, "who thanked his history professor for explaining World War I, saying, 'I've always wondered why people kept talking about a *second* world war.' "

One is not taught ignorance within the walls of American higher education. One comes equipped with it, a dowry of a sort from parents who haven't the energy or commitment to encourage reading at home, and a public school system that is underfinanced, overly politicized, and staffed with too few people who are either competent or dedicated, much less both. This being the case, what colleges and universities try to do, at least in some cases, is function like hospitals, providing the proper diagnoses for entering students and then prescribing whatever treatment might prove efficacious at so late a stage of their illnesses.

All too often, though, these schools call to mind the hospitals in the meat-grinder fiction of Robin Cook, where, to put it mildly, sinister forces are at work. Organs are stolen, viruses injected into healthy bloodstreams, and plagues actively developed. The institutions are not only failing to cure the disease, they are spreading it; not only spreading it, but incubating new strains. In the past decade and a half, the following courses have been available at major domiciles of higher learning in the United States:

"Rock 'n' Roll Is Here to Stay" (Brown); "Poets Who Sing" (Washington University); "Principles of Recreation" (Auburn); "Adjusting to a University" (Temple); "Sociology of Sociability" (Vassar); "Basic Roller Skating" and "Advanced Roller Skating" (Kent State); "Billiards, Bowling" (University of Iowa); "Ultimate Frisbee" (University of Massachusetts); "Rhythmic Activities" (University of Maryland); and " Black Hair as Culture and History" (Stanford).

At the University of North Carolina, one could sign up for "Applied Social Theory and Qualitative Social Research Methodology," a course with a nicely ponderous academic ring to it. But according to Charles Sykes in *The Hollow Men,* the course's nickname is "Deadhead 101," and its "materials consist of Grateful Dead cassettes and reviews of past shows. Students are required to attend Grateful Dead concerts to 'observe the subculture that surrounds the band.' " The purchase of T-shirts and souvenir programs, one assumes, was optional.

At the same time that classes like these were being offered, those that required serious books to be read and thoughtful papers to be written were being dropped from curriculums like so many discarded theories, or else were not being demanded of students in most fields of study. Some were perceived as no longer relevant, others as unfair to groups with various vested interests, which is to say that although they had stood the test of time, they had failed to qualify under the guidelines of current academic faddism. Says Dinesh D'Souza in *Illiberal Education*: "Research indicates that it is possible to graduate from 37 percent of American colleges without taking any courses in history, from 45 percent without taking a course in American or English literature, from 62 percent without studying any philosophy, and from 77 percent without studying a foreign language."

D'Souza published *Illiberal Education* in 1991; it is perhaps true that the figures are no longer so stark. However, this does not change the fact that millions of college students in the eighties received their diplomas with insufficient exposure to written language in its most elevating forms.

Take Brooke Shields. Model, actress, attendee of Andre Agassi tennis matches—she is perceived as one of the young intellectuals of the show business world because she earned a degree from Princeton. Yet as Thomas Sowell points out in *Inside American Education,* the word "earned" may be a bit grand. Sowell says that Shields took not so much as a single course in history, economics, biology, mathematics, chemistry, government, or sociology. Which raises the plaintive question: what did the young lady major in? Avoidance? It is as if Shields had signed up for a summer at Outward Bound, then gotten through it without fording a stream, camping out overnight, or even eating a bag of trail mix.

In 1966, more than half of all college freshmen in the United States checked a book out of the campus library for a reason other than a direct assignment. Twenty-five years later, the figure had dropped 25 percent. The American Library Association's Presidential Committee on Information Literacy has found that, "About one out of every four undergraduates spends no time in the library during a normal week, and 65 percent use the library four hours or less each week."

Appreciating literature, it seems, is no longer in vogue. It has gone the way of swallowing goldfish and stuffing Volkswagens among those so often referred to as the future of the United States.

But it gets worse. Not only do colleges spread the disease and incubate new strains; in some cases, they insist that the maladies are actually salubrious, the fevered brow more accurately thought of as the warm glow of health. Take the school of literary criticism known as deconstructionism.

The *Encyclopaedia Britannica* says that, according to the deconstructionist view, "meaning inheres in the world independently of any human attempt to represent it in words. It follows from this that the meaning of a text bears only accidental relationship to the author's conscious intentions."

Accidental relationship? The author, far from having the power assigned to him by Tocqueville, is a *bystander* in the literary process? Only according to so preposterous a line of thought as deconstructionism, which, as the word suggests, is the business of taking apart, tearing down, dismantling. It holds that all literary power belongs to the reader, who for that reason, is not bound either to understand or learn from the writer, or even to acknowledge that the writer is capable of instructing. As quoted earlier in this book, novelist Robertson Davies says that the reader completes the writer's scenario; deconstructionists believe the reader begins it, as well. Never mind that the pages of a book are covered by a multitude of tiny black figures in a variety of shapes and sizes; to a deconstructionist, every page is a tabula rasa, to be filled in by the perceptions, or misperceptions, of each individual who confronts it.

If Gulliver had come across a university in his travels, decon-

143

structionism would have been at the core of its curriculum. If there had been a branch campus in Orwell's Oceania, it would have hosted international deconstructionist symposia and published papers by the score. It is as if mathematicians had suddenly decided that two and two don't necessarily equal four anymore, but whatever the student concludes they equal; as if architects had suddenly announced that the floor plans of their dwellings meant nothing—the inhabitants could go to the bathroom in the foyer, eat their dinners in the garage, pass their nights in the kitchen.

It is not easy to understand the popularity of a theory so contrary to reason, although the current academic emphasis on diversity has something to do with it. Deconstructionism, you see, insists that a book has enough meanings to accommodate all its readers, so that no single reader's interpretation is wrong. Thus a person who misses every single point an author makes over the course of several hundred pages—who confuses the characters' motivations, misunderstands the importance of setting, finds symbolism where none exists and no symbolism where it is fairly bursting from the page—even this person is entitled to think as highly of his perceptions as is one whose comprehension has illuminated a work's subtlest nuance.

This indicates that the current academic emphasis on self-esteem also has something to do with deconstructionism's fashionability, self-esteem now being regarded as a genetic trait rather than the byproduct of honest accomplishment. Deconstructionism is a field that welcomes everyone, a social club with no standards for membership. Toward the author it is almost resentful, toward the reader warm and cuddly and positively virtuous in its non-judgmentalism.

One of the school's best known proponents is Stanley Fish, chairman of the English Department at Duke University. He explains the blessings that descend upon those who read decon-

144

structively: "Perhaps the greatest gift that falls to us is a greatly enhanced sense of the importance of our activities. No longer is the critic the humble servant of texts whose glories exist independently of anything he might do; it is what he does, within the restraints embedded in the literary institution, that brings texts into being and makes them available for analysis and appreciation."

Except that there are no restraints. The deconstructionist runs through his books like an anarchist through the corridors of reason and order, hurling invective, scattering garbage, spray-painting meaningless, if obtusely polysyllabic, slogans on the walls. And that suggests yet another reason for deconstructionism's appeal: it caters to a generation that sees no value in discipline, for either self or society. It holds that all writers are an oppressor class and all readers are to be rewarded for their long years of painful servitude by being allowed to confiscate the intellectual property that is the printed page and then to trash it with their diminished critical faculties.

It has gone so far as this: A few years ago, and presumably with a straight face, a British academic named A. W. McHoul thumbed his way through a volume of Pierre Reverdy's *Selected Poems*. He jotted down the first line he came upon in one verse, the second line in another, the third in a third, and so on, until he had assembled fourteen lines of poetry from fourteen different poems, a sonnet for the New Age illiterate. This process, in McHoul's words, yielded an "experimental text" which read as follows:

> The world is my prison
> Nothing new under the yellow sun
> The storm is calmed too late
> The lamp is a heart emptying itself
> The earth holds itself still

145

Part Two: Present

The pavement the sidewalks the distance
    the railings are white
If the door opens
The earth turns no more
This pale season
Of the attic or of paradise
When the eyes drip like blades of grass
Everybody there stares
They are still back there
Calling back your life

"This randomly constructed poem," McHoul explained,

had for our experimental purposes several advantages over an "actual" poem. It had no author with a possibly research-able/knowable biography. There was no person who "intended" this poem as it stands. The poem was not written for its sensi-ble character "as a piece." No person ever had the "intention" of any reader seeing any connection between these lines. In short, it was never "authored," "intended as sensible," "ratio-nally conceived," "publicly distributed," and the rest.

To repeat: Deconstructionist McHoul believed that these were the poem's *advantages.*

More than two thousand years ago, the written word was an object of suspicion among people who could not figure out how it got from the page to the inner recesses of the mind. In modern times, on some college campuses, it does not seem to be making the journey as often as it should.

The serious reader sometimes finds herself trapped in the empty occupations of the post-productive society. She polishes the images of politicians or writes the ad slogans for light beer or con-

146

ducts market feasibility studies for fast-food restaurants or crunches the numbers for supermarket coupon campaigns or refines the actuarial tables for insurance companies or runs leadership seminars for insufficiently vicious corporate executives or performs cosmetic surgery on perfectly acceptable-looking human beings or advises narcissistic lovers on their sexual techniques or formulates the play lists for oldies radio stations or negotiates the book deals for trendy chefs or writes feature articles for the style sections of tabloid newspapers or interviews actors about the social significance of their latest movies—and she justly fears that she is making little contribution either to self or society in the process.

So the serious reader is driven to literature. She flees to it, ensconces herself, homing in on its large truths and its carefully observed details, on its purposefully crafted characters and its vivid locales, on its psychological twistings and its resolutions of emotional turmoil. Thus does the reader retreat from pointlessness, bringing to her leisure hours a sense of meaning absent from the practice of employment. "The known is finite," biologist T. H. Huxley wrote, "the unknown infinite; intellectually we stand on an islet in the midst of an illimitable ocean of inexplicability. Our business in every generation is to reclaim a little more land, to add something to the extent and solidity of our possessions."

If she cannot reclaim the land through her work, the reader will try through her books.

The serious reader in the age of technology is aware of his limits. He is, after all, only himself, a single human being living at single moments in time, and the disadvantages of this condition are legion.

So much of what has happened in the world happened before the reader was born; he compensates by reading history, and acquaints himself with Thomas Carlyle on the French Revolution, Frederick Turner on the American frontier, and Bruce Catton on the Civil War.

So much is happening now, but in places far away and not easily understood; he compensates by reading geography and current events, and learns the lay of Micronesia according to P. F. Kluge, the Middle East according to Thomas Friedman, and Bosnia according to David Rieff.

So many people he has never met have achieved great feats of scholarship, imagination, and valor, or have lived lives so ignoble as to be contrarily instructive; he reads biography, and numbers among his intimates George Gershwin as seen by Edward Jablonski, Al Capone as seen by Laurence Bergreen, and Henry Louis Mencken as seen by William Manchester and Fred Hobson and a host of others.

So much of life will never be lived at all in the narrowly literal universe of the five senses; he reads fiction, and establishes a presence for himself in the epics of James Michener and the miniatures of Anne Tyler, in the cities of Saul Bellow and the suburbs of John Cheever, in the salons of Gore Vidal and the playing fields and Parisian cafes of Irwin Shaw. "Considering history as a moral exercise," Thomas Jefferson said, "her lessons would be too infrequent if confined to real life." The man who could not live without his books continued:

> We are therefore wisely framed to be as warmly interested for a fictitious as for a real personage. The spacious field of imagination is thus laid open to our use, and lessons may be formed to illustrate and carry home to the mind every moral rule of life. Thus a lively and lasting sense of filial duty is more effectually impressed on the mind of a son or daughter by King Lear, than by all the dry volumes of ethics and divinity that ever were written.

148

So the serious reader, like a child at play, has imaginary friends. But they raise real issues, and in doing so bind the reader more strongly to the nobler traditions of his culture than do any number of real friends with the vast sweep of their imaginary issues.

The serious reader delights in the company of his books. Their mute presence reassures him, eases his mind, invigorates him. "I am no sooner come into the library," theologian Robert Burton tells us of the favorite room in his house, "but I bolt the door, excluding lust, ambition, avarice. . . . In the lap of eternity, amongst so many divine souls, I take my seat with so lofty a spirit and sweet content."

The reader runs his eyes over his volumes, takes them in as, obeying his designs, they crowd into one another on his shelves and climb the walls. He smiles as if looking at a natural wonder, and why not? His books are the wonder of *his* nature, each a keepsake of inestimable value: a snapshot of an old friend, a diary entry of an enriching experience, a postcard from a place like no other on earth. Books are memories made tangible, and surrounded by them, like a web of his own intricate weaving, the reader manages to confound the rapid transit of the years, the frantic pace of the days.

For a time, none were more frantic than mine. As a television newsman, my life was a neverending blur of hotel rooms and airplane cabins, of destinations I could no longer distinguish from one another and food that defied the powers of my digestive juices. I had enough frequent flyer miles for a trip to Alpha Centauri, as well as the world's largest collection of scratch cards for giveaways at fast food restaurants. I never knew when I would wake up or when I would go to sleep or *where* I would go to sleep. I only knew that, awake, I would be chasing politicians or bad-gering survivors, begging cops for information or experts for analysis, trying to understand book burners or corporate raiders or serial rapists, and on more than one occasion jogging around a parking garage at midnight hoping to find my car, which was the fifth one I had rented that week in five different cities, so I couldn't even remember what color it was, let alone the make and model. My heartbeat thundered, my stomach churned. I struggled to breathe, was unable to focus either my eyes or my brain. I made my deadlines, always made my deadlines, but always faced a new set tomorrow—and the hour hands spun around like second hands; digital clocks clattered with the constant flipping of numbers. I was twentieth-century man; hear me gasp.

And then in the midst of it all, I would find myself at home for a day or two, tossed aside, events done with me for the time being. I would sleep for ten or eleven or twelve hours, and then stumble out of bed and take to my library. I would find, as Sven Birkerts does in *The Gutenberg Elegies,* that I was reviving myself through "an exchange in which we hand over our groundedness in the here and now in order to take up groundedness in the elsewhere of the book. The more fully we can accomplish this, the more truly we can be said to be reading. The tree in front of us must dim so that the tree on the page can take on outline and presence. The operation is by no means passive; we collude at every point. We will that it be so."

But I would not settle for mere reading; rather, I would hook myself up to a book as if it were a biofeedback device. Maybe Henry David Thoreau's *Walden* or Paul Theroux's travelogues or even something by Edith Wharton or Henry James. Nineteenth-century sensibilities; feel them soothe. I would breathe deeply, then let loose: in and out, in and out, easy does it and even easier. For a moment or two I might close my eyes. All thoughts but those inspired by the book would vanish, all ties to lands outside its covers dissolve.

The results were immediately apparent. My blood pressure dropped. My brain waves settled and my heart began to beat more slowly. My stomach calmed, shoulder muscles unknotted, and my soul, if it did not necessarily take wing each time I wired myself into the library, at least lightened enough to make the notion of ascent seem possible. All my senses were regulated, all my clocks were sundials. British philosopher Jeremy Rifkin believed that "Every religion holds forth the prospect of defeating time, escaping time, overcoming time, reissuing time, or denying time altogether."

So does every book.

Yes, *all* the senses are regulated, all on full alert.

The reader takes a deep breath in her library and fills her head with the venerable scent of books, which to the child Ray Bradbury was "like imported spices," and to others has seemed almost a musk, earthy and basic.

The reader touches in her library, taking Winston Churchill's advice to "handle, or as it were, fondle [the books]—peer into them, let them fall open where they will, read from the first sentence that arrests the eye, set them back on their shelves with your own hands, arrange them on your own plan. . . . Let them be your friends; let them at any rate be your acquaintances."

The reader listens in her library, noting a prickly quality to the silence, as if the sounds from the outside world were being filtered not through an extra foot of wall space, but through a unique sensibility.

So diligently is the reader attuned to the room that she is even aware of changes taking place under the dust jackets and inside the covers, changes subtle yet unmistakable. She picks up *The Fountainhead*: Howard Roark has grown colder over the years, more inflexible, his principles simply too much at odds with the raw materials of human nature; blowing up the housing development is not egoism, as Ayn Rand approvingly defines the term, but megalomania. Perhaps Roark can still be admired from afar, but the feeling can no longer withstand proximity.

She picks up *The Catcher in the Rye*: Holden Caulfield has grown petulant, selfish, becoming less a spokesman for a generation than a rather ineloquent voice pleading in the dark for his own gratification.

She picks up *The Great Gatsby*: Nick Carraway has grown obsequious. "I'm inclined to reserve all judgments," he says, but that does not make him impartial, only submissive; and as he ceaselessly, nonjudgmentally attaches himself to Gatsby and Daisy and the rest of their crowd, he seems like a groupie in the wake of a rock band, a literary character who alarmingly foreshadows the mentality of the coming celebrity culture.

On the other hand, she picks up *The Mosquito Coast*: Alfie Fox has mellowed with time, or perhaps it is more accurate to say that his erratic flight to Central America seems more comprehensible now than it once did, as the social institutions he abhorred in the United States continue to crumble, and as behavior deteriorates and good taste becomes ever more a matter of irrelevance. Alfie thought his native land was turning into "a dopetaking, doorlocking ulcerated danger zone of rabid scavengers and criminal millionaires and moral sneaks. And look at the schools, And look at the politicians. . . . And there were people in New York City who lived on pet food, who would kill you for a little loose change." In 1982, when Paul Theroux created him, Alfie Fox seemed excessive. A decade and some change later, he could be writing editorials for a perfectly respectable urban daily.

There is within the walls of the library, then, a population in a constant state of flux. There is growth and agitation, renewal and dissolution. The reader's imaginary friends are returning the favor of his companionship by providing him with a means of keeping constant check on his own values and interests.

The library is not, as some would have it, a place for the retiring of disposition or faint of heart. It is not an ivory tower or a quiet room in a sanitarium facing away from the afternoon sun. It is, rather, a command center, a power base. A board room, a war room. An Oval Office for all who preside over their own destinies. One does not retreat from the world here; one prepares to join it at an advantage.

George Washington, not a true lover of the literary arts, nonetheless readied himself for an early command against the British by hunkering down with "five books—military."

Napoleon went to war with hundreds of volumes in his arsenal; to Waterloo he brought seventy by Voltaire alone, perhaps becoming *too* concerned with matters beyond the day-to-day.

As a boy in Kansas, Dwight Eisenhower preferred reading to farming, so his mother hid the family books. Dwight found them, so his mother locked them in the cupboard with the liquor. Dwight picked the lock, so his mother gave up, allowing him the inebriation of the printed page, the young man, among other accomplishments, memorizing all of Hannibal's Carthaginian strategies and maneuvers.

Eisenhower's eventual vice president was just as avid a reader. His younger brother Ed, though, saw no particular charms in written language, and this troubled Richard Nixon. Hoping to change Ed's mind, Nixon sent home letters from his naval base in the South Pacific, making an offer. "I'll give you ten cents for every ten pages you read." It worked. When big brother got home from the Second World War, little brother collected three hundred dollars.

Churchill even found time to fondle and arrange his books as the Luftwaffe bombed London in the war's bleakest moments. Some people thought he was shirking duty. Not so. He was taking heart.

And who knows how many other men and women, their names escaping posterity, have equipped themselves for either combat or peace in the enriching redoubts of literature? Who knows how many have attained the extraordinary or at least conquered the mundane, found homes in which to dwell or at least set up temporary housekeeping in structures prepared for them by authors who were long and meticulous at their labors? Who knows how many have raised possibilities, and how far those possibilities have taken them?

A century ago, cigars were made by hand and the men who did the work led far from invigorating lives. The pay was adequate, but the hours were long and the tasks so numbingly tedious that even to summarize them in clipped phrases is to paint a detailed portrait of early industrial monotony. Render leaves, sort leaves, spray leaves with flavorings. Remove midrib, apply binder leaf, encase leaf in wrapper. Paste head, cut cigar to proper length, fasten wrapper with putty of gum tragacanth. Then do it again for the next cigar and again for the next. Do it hundreds of times a day, thousands of times a week, millions of times in a life—render and sort and spray, remove and apply and encase, paste and cut and fasten, all the while sitting at tables in factories so poorly lighted that the workdays seemed a perpetual dusk, and so poorly ventilated that the air collected about the men in pools, like the fetid, unmoving water of a swamp.

But the cigarmakers were not alone at their tasks. A hundred years before, the French had formed clubs known as *veillée* and the Germans clubs known as *Spinnstube*; when they met, the men would repair tools and the women mend clothes and the children play in silence while someone read aloud from one of the popular books of the day. The cigarmakers seem to have taken a cue from these groups, hiring readers of their own. For the most part, they were young men who had not been successful at finding other jobs, but prizing literature above income anyhow, were happy enough to be paid a few cents to read books even in so foul an atmosphere. They read to the cigarmakers of grander lives, and the cigarmakers dreamed; they read to them of sorrier experiences, and the cigarmakers gave thanks for their relative good fortune; they read to them of different ages, and the cigarmakers simply reflected, sailing away from the demands of reality, the reports of the senses, and stretching the otherwise cramped muscles of their imagination. It was another outbreak of the oral tradition, this time in the heyday of robber baron capitalism.

Render, sort, spray.

He laid down his fifteen cents and crept off with weary steps to his allotted room. It was a dingy affair, wooden, dusty, hard. A small gas jet furnished sufficient light for so rueful a corner.
"Hm," he said, clearing his throat and locking the door.

Remove, apply, encase.

Now he began tentatively to take off his clothes, but stopped first with his coat and tucked it along the crack under the door. His vest he arranged in the same place. His old wet cracked hat he laid softly upon the table, then he pulled off his shoes and lay down.

Paste, cut, fasten.

It seemed as if he thought awhile for now he arose and turned the gas out, standing calmly in the blackness, hidden from view.

After a few moments in which he reviewed nothing, but merely hesitated, he turned the gas on again, but applying no match. Even then he stood there, hidden wholly in that kindness which is night, while the uprising fumes filled the room. When the odor reached his nostrils he quit his attitude and fumbled for the bed.

"What's the use," he said wearily, as he stretched himself to rest.

And so the suicide of the tycoon Hurstwood, ultimately so poor a man, as Carrie Meeber, the street girl who had been his mistress, turns her back on him and achieves success on the stage. The cigarmakers were extremely fond of Theodore Dreiser, and found *Sister Carrie* especially poignant.

But it was not just the men in the factories who needed the sustenance of literary art; it was the women at home, trapped in their own modes of workday misery, as dubious as the men at times about the promises that America had made them.

By history's lights, Rose Cohen was no one special; she could have been anyone's daughter, a cigarmaker's wife. But in *Literacy in the United States,* Katherine Tinsley and Carl Kaestle tell us that "Rose read stories to escape the Jewish ghetto of New York in the 1890s. She discovered that one could rent books from soda-water dealers for a few pennies, and she started reading one each week. 'I now lived in a wonderful world. One time I was a beautiful countess living unhappily in a palace, another time I was a beggar's daughter singing in the street.' "

Tinsley and Kaestle continue,

Farther south in Tennessee, Lillian Spurrier escaped her kitchen duties to her ultimate betterment. She lived with her two daughters in her mother's house. One day in 1904 she became so absorbed in *The Prisoner of Zenda* that she forgot to take a cake from the oven. When her mother scolded her about the wasted provisions, Lillian determined to move out, take up photography, and make enough money so she would never again feel chagrined over something so simple as a burnt cake. Her daughter wrote in her autobiography, "For years afterward, whenever we had a specially good dinner or got new dresses, Mother would say, 'We have the Prisoner of Zenda to thank for that.' "

At about the same time that Lillian Spurrier was ruining her cake, Mary Antin, whose Russian parents had immigrated to New England, was reading her way through the shelves of the Boston Public Library. Among her favorite works were the Horatio Alger stories and the novels of Louisa May Alcott, but she was indiscriminate in her tastes, unstinting in her appreciation. Years later she would write an autobiography called *The Promised Land,* and recall the magical day when she not only departed from the library but emerged as well "from the dim places where the torch of history has never been, creeping slowly into the light of civilized existence, pushing more steadily forward to the broad plateau of modern life."

Men and women who trust to books in the age of technology hold no special charms. They are as likely as anyone else to feel adrift from time to time, as likely to know the void of unanswered questions, the pain of unfulfilled ambitions, the waste of unspoken sentiments. But others may have nowhere to turn. The serious reader always has a place of his own.

EPILOGUE

FUTURE

Illustration from *Le chemin des écoliers* (Paris: Librairie de L. Hachette, 1861), p. 188.

*I*t is an afternoon in the spring of 1995, and my son walks past me with his hands in his pockets and a book under his arm, whistling tonelessly, faking nonchalance. He waves the book at me, just a flash, then grins and keeps going. *Peter Pan* by Sir James M. Barrie, his father's childhood edition. Some of the gatherings have pulled away from the spine and the spine itself is cracked; the once-vivid colors on the cover have gone monochromatic and the corners are bent back and frayed. The book, in other words, has not done well by the years. But what about the story?

"You're really going to read it?" I say.

"I've *been* reading it." He is still walking.

"You could've told me."

He shrugs, cocks his head as if about to tell me to chill.

"So what do you think?"

"Later, Dad," he says; maybe the nonchalance is real.

He tugs at the front door of our house, opens it and shuffles outside. He crosses the yard, climbs a small hill, and deposits himself under a dogwood tree that has not yet begun to bloom, curling into its bowed trunk. This is where he goes with his books sometimes. This is a place of his own. On the spring day of which I write, my only son and senior child is ten years old and counting.

161

Epilogue: Future

He does not immediately attend to the book. For a moment or two he pulls up blades of grass and holds them in his palm. He blows on them and watches as they scatter in the light breeze. Then for a few more moments, he raises his face to the sky, so pale today that it seems to have aged no less than the cover of *Peter Pan.* The sun has just passed its zenith and is frozen for the time being, as if unwilling to continue yet one more descent toward one more evening. A few clouds drift across it idly, throwing down shadows and then sweeping them up again. My son closes his eyes and shakes his head; there is no way to guess what he is thinking. When his eyes open again, they are wider than before.

He reaches for a low-hanging branch of the dogwood, yanking it toward him and letting it spring back up. There may be a few buds on it, but I can't tell; that might be a robin's nest wedged into the corner at the trunk, but I'm not sure. In fact, from my vantage point at the living room window, I can barely make out the branch at all; after it springs into place again, it becomes just one more streak in the sky, taking a position in the thick, black rows of power lines and telephone wires that attach our neighborhood to the age of information. One line atop another atop another atop another. Lines hanging over the curbs on both sides of the street, then crossing it in two or three places at a diagonal. Lines reminding me of musical staves on which no one has yet written a note.

But not all of the lines run parallel to their mates. A few shoot away at sharp angles, into and out of transformers, on and off the huge poles that have been erected solely to support them. The poles are tall, the dogwood tree short. The poles are ramrod straight, altogether imposing, the tree bent and a little timorous in present company. And the branches are stumpy, while the power lines are long and sleek and run off into the distance as far as the eye can see.

My son brings up his legs and pitches his head forward so that his chin rests on his knees. He holds the book at his ankles with both hands and opens it, forearms squeezing against his calves. What a position! Of course, I could have assumed it when I was his age. I could even assume it now for a few seconds, two or three; then I would tumble onto my side and scream for 911. Toby Burns, you see, is more supple than his father. And his eyes are better and his curiosity greater and his spirit more receptive to myth and fable—and those are only a few of the differences between us as child charts a course through Sir James M. Barrie's *Peter Pan* about four decades after parent first made the trip.

He flips through the book, finds his place, bores in. But does he take off, soar out of sight of all who are earthbound? Does he circle Big Ben, plow through clouds, all the rest? Maybe. His concentration certainly seems complete. He pays no attention to the squirrel scampering across the lawn in front of him, or to the game of four-square that has just begun at the corner. Nor does he look wistfully at the house across the street, where one of his friends is sure to be playing a video game this fine spring afternoon, probably the one in which a character named Death Seeker tries to rip out the heart of a character named Cobra Breath, and then twist off Cobra Breath's head and stuff the heart down his neck while Cobra Breath's bloody guts ooze out through his ribs and turn into a slimy gel that drips down his legs into a fiery puddle on the ground. Or something like that. Death Seeker then goes on either to save the world or destroy it; I can't remember the value system of this particular game, or the point totals that reward success at the more difficult levels.

In *Peter Pan,* by Sir James M. Barrie, Captain Hook is described as wearing "his hair in long curls, which at a little distance looked like black candles." I wonder what color Death Seeker's hair is. The pirate's eyes were "forget-me-not blue," except "when he was plunging his hook into you, at which time two red spots appeared in them and lit them up horribly." I wonder whether Cobra Breath gets red spots in his eyes when he tries to protect himself from Death Seeker's onslaught. Which is to say: I wonder whether anyone can possibly take the menace of James Hook seriously in an age when each new generation of computer graphics portrays decapitation and bloodletting so much more grotesquely than the preceding one, and when thousands of men and women are devoting hundreds of thousands of hours to turning out even more advanced generations of computer graphics, at the same time that thousands of other men and women are devoting hundreds of thousands of their own hours to marketing these video games to kids who will play them until their eyes crust over and their jaws hang slack and a book seems so lifelessly unengaging an object to them that they do not even want one in their rooms, much less taking up space in what remains of their conscious minds.

I put my foot up on the window ledge and cross my forearms over my thighs. I fiddle with my glasses, let out a sigh. I can almost hear the hum of the power lines over Toby's head, can almost see them vibrate as they stretch from pole to pole, neighborhood to neighborhood, nation to nation.

I don't know why I held onto my old copy of *Peter Pan*. I did not intend it to play an important role in a period of adult rumination, nor did I dream of handing the book over to my son when he reached a certain age, making it into a rite of passage. In fact, I didn't even know I *had* kept the book; I simply came across it a few years ago in a box containing an assortment of items from my early years. There was a first baseman's mitt with the name Eddie Waitkus stamped on it, some 45 rpm records on the long-defunct Fee-Bee and Specialty labels, and a collection of term papers I wrote in my junior and senior years of high school. The glove was mildewed, the records warped, and the papers so full of blather that I could barely stand to read them, even after granting myself a dispensation for youth and inexperience.

But the book, although battered and dusty, somehow managed to produce memories that were sharply focused, in virtual mint condition. I was amazed. So many years had passed since I last read *Peter Pan*—so many people and places had intruded, so many events, so many jobs and the demands that went along with them—and yet so much came back to me so quickly. I took the book out of the box, wiped it with a paper towel, and gripped it in both hands. I looked at it for a few seconds, just looked at it. Did not riffle the pages, did not have to, for I found myself remembering, almost as if telepathically, what had once been so familiar. I remembered the lost boy named Tootles shooting "the Wendy" with his arrow, and then learning to his horror that his victim was a lady, not a bird. I remembered the wonderful cave where the lost boys lived, "rough and simple, and not unlike what baby bears would have made of an underground house in the same circumstances." I remembered the ferocious battle, dryly described as a "brush on the lagoon," which brought the lost boys and the Indians together, making them into the allies they should have been all along.

But even more surprising was that I could still recall the feelings the book had once evoked in me. I could not reproduce them, you understand; there is no way that childhood emotional responses can survive so powerful a solvent as adult sensibilities, and I have been riddled with the latter for longer than I care to admit. But I could bring the feelings back on an intellectual level, could sort them into categories and affix the proper labels to them, and that by itself seemed an accomplishment of some magnitude. *Exhilaration*—when Peter rescued Wendy from Hook's vile clutches, "advancing upon him through the air with dagger

165

poised." *Melancholy*—when Peter and the Darling kids went their separate ways a few pages later. *Titillation*—when I considered the prospect, however remote in the world unregulated by authors, of eternal childhood.

What I do not remember is the decision to present *Peter Pan* to my son. When did I make it? What was I thinking? In his review of *The Wind in the Willows* many years ago, A. A. Milne said that the book "is a test of character." Did I want to make *Peter Pan* a similar test for Toby? If so, how would I grade it? By what standards? By what *right*? After all, I grew up in an era when married couples on television programs could not be shown to sleep in the same bed. Toby grows up in an era when *un*married couples go shopping for condoms. I grew up when cartoon characters bonked each other on the head with rubber chickens. As he grows up, they are farting in each other's faces and cackling at the sheer drollery of it.

My era: Elvis Presley sings, "Jus' wanna be your teddy bear. Put a chain aroun' muh neck, an' lead me anywhere."

His era: Green Day sings, "I'm so damn bored I'm going blind!!! And I smell like shit!"

My era: *Pillow Talk* hints at sex and grosses a few million dollars.

His era: *Disclosure* fills the screen with sex, discloses everything, and takes in more money in a week than most Third World countries accumulate in a year. And then there is *Pulp Fiction*'s brutality and *Higher Learning*'s vulgarity and *Dumb and Dumber*'s utter tastelessness, which at some points descends to such a bottom-feeding nadir that when *those* characters fart, the tone of the entire movie improves.

More about the culture in the time of Toby Burns, as filtered through the perceptions of his father: The coolest kids in public schools emulate the speech patterns of the brain-dead, the clothing styles of the homeless, and the cynicism of vice cops. The teachers emulate the kids. Something called virtual reality emulates reality-without-the-adjective and somehow seems superior to it, thus giving further evidence of the glorification of the ersatz which lies at the core of most technological progress. Computers are becoming as common in the home as electric can openers, and are being hooked up to telephone networks and e-mail systems and CD-ROM players and fax machines and photocopiers and maybe even pizza ovens, for all I know—the whole blessed gridwork of wires and boxes and high-tech innards designed to move isolated little globules of data so quickly that the very idea of contemplation now seems a weakness of character, and no one even thinks anymore to question the relationship between means and ends.

And then there's this guy at his living room window, Creature from Another Era, looking out at his son and musing on what the lad will make of so old-fashioned a thing as a book, and in particular of so old-fashioned a book as *Peter Pan,* which was written by someone who has a "Sir" in front of his name. There he is, this guy with a personal library that consists of exactly no videotapes, precisely zero CD-ROMS, a grand total of zilch in the way of computer programs and laserdiscs—and roughly 2,300 codices, of all things! Some are on shelves and some are on tables and some are in boxes, but regardless of location the guy has read virtually every single one of them, trying to make up for what happened in the world before he was born and what happens now but far away and what will never happen at all as far as the records of journalism are concerned. He even re-reads a few of the books from time to time, so that he still finds Thomas Hardy heartwrenching and Victor Hugo soul-stirring and Ayn Rand mindexpanding. He is still spooked by Edgar Allan Poe, intrigued by Sir Arthur Conan Doyle, confounded by Jules Verne. He still knows the anguish of Fyodor Dostoevsky and the irreverence of Mark Twain and the sentimentality of Charles Dickens. He stands at the window of his house, this anachronism in modern garb, and you can see it in his eyes: he prefers a Barnes & Noble superstore to a Blockbuster Video, a Winston Groom novel to a Robert Zemeckis movie, a walk in the woods to a double-feature of PBS nature documentaries.

And yet he has a son—not to mention an even younger daughter—who is coming of age in the United States of America a mere five years before the onset of century number twenty-one.

What kind of father *is* this guy, anyhow?

A week or two later, another of my son's places: the room he calls home on the top floor of our house, which he has furnished according to eclectic tastes and specific dreams. Toby dreams, for example, of being an all-star in the NBA; glued to the back of his door is a Shaq Attaq backboard and hoop, the latter just large enough to accommodate a basketball the size and consistency of a grapefruit.

Toby dreams of being a soloist at Carnegie Hall; next to his dresser are a trumpet case and the sheet music he will play at his school's spring concert next week.

He dreams of being a writer; on top of the dresser are the notebooks in which he sets down his short stories and tall tales and biographical sketches and essays and song lyrics and multigenerational epics of fantasy and adventure.

He dreams of being an artist; other notebooks on the dresser contain his sketches of creatures that breathe fire and the castles erected by mere mortals to repel the monsters' advances.

He dreams of being a chess master; on his desk is a trade magazine open to an analysis of the relative merits of the Benko Gambit versus the Meran variation.

He dreams of being a historian; taped to one of the walls are copies of the Declaration of Independence and the Constitution, as well as a poster of American Presidents and a compilation of the "Golden Sayings of Abraham Lincoln."

He dreams of being a world traveler; on the facing wall are *National Geographic* maps of places he vows to know intimately one day: Italy, Greece, Australia, the Nile Valley.

What my son does not dream of is neatness. Toby makes his bed less often than the center for the Orlando Magic makes foul shots, and today the sheets are pulled out from the bottom of the mattress, the pillows are mashed against the wall, and an old Gund bear is wedged between the pillows. The books in Toby's bookcase appear to have been thrown, not arranged, and the whole structure tilts forward at so precarious an angle that it threatens to topple at any moment, causing an avalanche of literature, model airplanes, and souvenir hockey pucks. And the top of his desk is virtually invisible; in addition to the chess magazine, there are boxes of crayons and markers and pens and pencils, a pencil sharpener shaped like a panda, a tape dispenser and stapler, stacks of construction paper and a pair of scissors, a bottle of glue, a file box for index cards, CDs by Pearl Jam and the Cranberries, audio-cassettes by Sting and Stone Temple Pilots, a set of headphones connected to nothing, and an old issue of *Sports Illustrated for Kids,* overdue at the library.

It is seven o'clock on a school night. Toby has asked me up for a chat. I do not know the topic. I assume it is not interior design.

"Dad," he says, as I push open the door, which swings the Shaq hoop over the dresser, almost toppling a soccer trophy sitting on a tissue box that itself sits atop the stack of notebooks that collect his voluminous prose stylings.

"Hi, pal."

"I have to tell you something." He is seated at his desk, having turned in the chair to face me.

169

I drop onto the bed, pushing aside some clumps of blanket and a damp washcloth. "What's that?"

"I want you to know that I'm really enjoying the book." He reaches under the *Sports Illustrated for Kids,* extracting *Peter Pan.*

"You are?"

Nod, nod, nod—and he smiles toothily as he brings the book up to the side of his face, the pose of a pitchman on the Home Shopping Channel.

"How far are you?"

"About halfway," he says, and narrows his eyes to gauge my reaction. "Do you think that's far enough?"

"Wherever you are is far enough."

"I know I've been going at it pretty slow lately, but I've had so much stuff for school, you know, with—"

I hold out a hand. "I'm just glad you're reading it at all. I know it's not the kind of book you would have chosen for yourself."

"I would've if I'd have known about it."

"Really?"

"Cross my heart." He leans the book against a crayon box.

I fall back on the bed and roll onto my side, wedging my elbow into the mattress, balancing my head in the palm of my hand. "What exactly do you like about it?" I say.

"The mood."

It is not what I had expected. "The mood?"

More nods. "See, what happens is, you open the book and start to read, and after you've been reading a while you get inside the story, almost like you're a character. Or at least like you're really there watching the characters close up, seeing them with your own eyes. And then you keep reading and you get in even deeper, because the book has this incredible feeling of welcomeness."

"But you don't feel it right away?"

170

He says he doesn't.

"How long does it take?"

"Well, when I first started reading the book, it took me a page or two every time to start to get comfortable. Now it's just a few paragraphs, or even sentences, so it's getting easier."

"What made it hard at first?"

"The way Barrie writes."

"How would you describe it?" I feel as if I'm back on television, interviewing someone who, having begun to confuse me with Ted Koppel or one of those, is already hoping that he never sees another microphone or camera as long as he lives.

"I would say . . ." Toby taps his finger against his front teeth a few times. "I would say it's real easy to tell the author's not alive anymore. I mean, he writes the way people used to write a long time ago. Sort of . . . corny."

"Corny?"

Toby pops out of his chair. "Not bad corny, not bad corny, don't get the wrong idea, Dad." He takes one hand in another, squeezes. "It's just not the kind of writing you see in books today, either the junky ones or the ones that win the Newbery Prize and all that."

"So would you like to read the same story in someone else's words? Do you wish R. L. Stine or Shel Silverstein had written *Peter Pan*?"

Toby's smile is slight, but enough to tell me that the question has caught his fancy; it is something he can play with, roll around in his head for a while. He backs up a step, folds his arms across his chest, and lets the while pass. Then he tells me, "I don't think so."

"Why not?"

"Because it wouldn't be the same story if another person did the writing. Not even if that person had identical characters doing

171

identical things in identical places. It would still be totally different because the mood wouldn't be the same."

"Why wouldn't it?"

"Geez, Dad."

"I'm overdoing this?"

"It's just that you already know all the answers."

"No, I don't. I know what *my* answers would be, but I have no
idea about yours."

A click of the tongue. "All right," he says, "but listen up. I'm
not going to repeat this."

I swear he won't have to.

He drops his derrière onto the desktop. "The words don't just
tell you what's happening in a story, they help you make up your
mind about it. They give you clues about whether you're supposed
to take things seriously or not or whether you're supposed to be
happy or sad or angry or whatever. And like I said, they create the
mood, and the mood's the most important part of the whole book,
the part that stays with you the longest. Okay?"

"Okay."

"Good," he says. "Now, when do I get to ask *you* some questions?"

I slide a pillow under my elbow, adjust the angle of my head.
"Ready when you are, pal."

Toby claps his hands. I fear a full-scale interrogation. Instead,
he says, "Actually, I think there's just one thing I want to know.
When you were a kid, you really liked *Peter Pan,* right?"

"Right."

"Have you read it since you were a grownup?"

I tell him I have.

"Did you like it as much as you used to?"

As a matter of fact I didn't, and it is a subject I've been rolling
around in my own head lately. Conclusion? Like Howard Roark

and Holden Caulfield and Nick Carraway and Alfie Fox before him, Peter Pan has changed over the years—a particular irony in view of the vows he swore never to grow up, never to yield to the depredations of maturity. True, Peter may have remained a child in chronological terms, but he has become more manipulative than I remember, less sensitive, cunning in a way. I concede that these are traits of the child no less than of the adult, but it seemed to me that Peter has developed them in full grownup measure. In particular, I refer to the heartache he causes Mr. and Mrs. Darling by kidnapping their children in the middle of the night, and to the total lack of remorse that he demonstrates for the deed. Peter does not suggest leaving a note to tell the mother and father where their kids have gone, does not send a message back from Neverland, and when Wendy tells her story on the island "about the feelings of the unhappy parents with all their children flown away," Peter is as unmoved as if he had been listening to a description of local flora and fauna.

As a boy, I was not bothered by this attitude. I can't even remember noticing it. As the father of Tobias and Cailin, I find it chilling. And as if to reinforce the notion that people who bear and raise children are unworthy of kindness from either the offspring themselves or anyone else on the planet, Sir James M. Barrie portrays the elder Darlings as coldly unpleasant human beings, almost caricatures. Mrs. Darling, for instance, has a "sweet mocking mouth"; there is "one kiss on it that Wendy could never get, although there it was, perfectly conspicuous in the right-hand corner."

And Mr. Darling, who cannot get the kiss either, "was one of those deep ones who know about stocks and shares. Of course, no one really knows, but he quite seemed to know, and he often said stocks were up and shares were down in a way that would have made any woman respect him."

No wonder Peter ran away from his own parents the day he

was born. And no wonder that when he finally agrees to escort the Darling kids home, he cannot resist a final show of disdain for their poor progenitors' misery, magically erecting a set of bars over the window of the children's bedroom. For the moment, younger ones are trapped outside, older ones within. "You will never see Wendy again, lady," Peter snarls at Mrs. Darling, and when he discovers that "two tears were sitting on her eyes," he merely becomes angry with her.

Peter changes his mind of course, and it does not take long. But he does so reluctantly, in low spirits.

> "Oh, all right," he said at last, and gulped. Then he unbarred the window. "Come on, Tink," he cried, with a frightful sneer at the laws of nature; "we don't want any silly mothers," and he flew away.

And so a further irony: I insist that the son I love read a book whose title character insists that my feeling not be reciprocated.

"I guess I didn't like the story as much as I did when I was your age," I tell him.

"Why not?"

"No more questions."

"Dad." He gives the word two syllables, extra emphasis on each, the way he always does when protesting a show of parental hypocrisy. But I will not be budged.

"How about you?" I say. "Was there anything you didn't like about the book?"

He frowns and shakes his head; he will not be budged either, will return to the topic of my revised opinion as soon as he believes the time is right. But for now: "A couple things," he allows.

"Tell me."

"Well, there's too much stuff in the beginning about what's happening in the house. You know, where the Darlings live in London? All the day-to-day details. You have to wait too long for Peter Pan to show up, and since that's when things really get going in the book, I think he should zip to the scene a lot sooner."

"What else?"

"I don't think Barrie does a very good job of explaining how a person can fly."

"What do you mean?"

"I marked this section," Toby says. "I wanted to show you. Here," and he picks up the book and hands it to me, telling me to slip out the orange card near the beginning. "It's the page on the left side. The third paragraph down, I think."

I read to myself.

> It looked delightfully easy, and they tried it first from the floor, and then from the beds, but they always went down instead of up.
>
> "I say, how do you do it?" asked John, rubbing his knee. He was quite a practical boy.
>
> "You just think lovely, wonderful thoughts," Peter explained, "and they lift you up in the air."

"See what I mean?" Toby says. " 'Lovely, wonderful thoughts,' and then all of a sudden you turn into an eagle or something. He needs to explain it better than that."

"But how can he?" I say. "People can't fly in real life. How is an author supposed to write about it as if it's possible?"

"I don't know." My son's voice shoots up half an octave. "That's *his* problem. But it's what he gets paid for. An author should be able to do anything if he puts his mind to it, and if he knows enough words and is a creative enough person. And Bar-

175

rie sure is, you can tell that from every other part of the book. I think he just got lazy in the flying part. There has to be a way to make it sound more official, like it's something that can really happen, even though it's totally out of the question. I mean, think of how an airplane flies, all that stuff about lift and drag, about how the air pressure's lower above the wing but stays the same beneath it, so this ten-ton machine can get up in the air and stay there as long as it wants. *That* sounds crazy when you first hear it, don't you think?"

I take off my glasses and pinch the bridge of my nose, turning away from him before I smile. My son, quite a practical boy himself. And such a good thing for a dreamer to be.

A Sunday afternoon two weeks later, and nobody home but me. My wife is teaching English to Spanish speakers; my son is riding his bike to a friend's house; my daughter is climbing the dogwood in the front yard as if she were tree-borne by nature, shimmying up the trunk, swinging from branches.

I am inside and sedentary, browsing through the *Washington Post Book World* on the living room sofa. I read Kathryn Harrison on Anne Tyler's *Ladder of Years,* Jonathan Yardley on Claire Tomalin's *Mrs. Jordan's Profession,* and Marie Arana-Ward on Deirdre Bair's *Anais Nin: A Biography.* Then I turn another page, and a piece of notebook paper flutters out of the magazine. A white sheet with faint green lines, sentences single-spaced and written in pencil in neat block letters. Another review—Toby Burns on Sir James M. Barrie's *Peter Pan*:

> The novel I just read was a truly fantastic story. This story had the biggest sense of imagination I've ever read. Clearly this book was made up, but if you were settled enough in the book you wouldn't know it! The book's a true, true masterpiece, it's

old but who said old was bad. In fact I think it's better because it's so different. You can get the modern world anywhere. This book was a phenomenally imaginative story.

This book is

PETER PAN!

Toby says nothing about the subversion of parental love, nothing to indicate that he thinks less of me than he used to, has begun to wish there were bars between us from time to time. I should tell the people in the Midwest about this, the ones who burned the books all those years ago. Maybe they'd feel better about things. Maybe not.

I fold my son's review in half and slip it into my shirt pocket. I ask myself what characters he will read about next. Probably not Bomba the Jungle Boy, who must be so politically incorrect by this time that his books have been hurled into dumpsters and ground back into pulp. Probably not Chip Hilton, whose girlfriends were all cheerleaders and his boyfriends all Caucasians; that would never do anymore. And probably not the Hardy Boys, who never solved a crime of social consciouslessness, never took a case of burning contemporary relevance, and that would never do either. Too bad; Toby might have enjoyed these people and their adventures. Or just as well; he might have learned an unhealthy degree of social stereotyping.

But it doesn't matter either way. I don't want my son to follow in my footsteps, only to stroll along the same broad thoroughfare. Once en route, he can make his own decisions: determine the pace he will keep, the detours he will choose, the landmarks and fellow travelers he will remember most fondly. All I want is the assurance that he is exposing himself to the energy of ideas, learning to thrive on it, being propelled by it, the assurance that he is expanding his circle of acquaintances, his knowledge of place, and his awareness of self. I want to know that, like some of the great heroes of classical fiction, Toby will set his sights on what is unattainable in life no less than what falls within easy reach, that he will miss subway stops when sufficiently engrossed, that he will become a figure of some standing in the community of books, joining his father and mother and millions of other men and women like them over hundreds and hundreds of years.

Well, maybe I'd like Toby to follow in a *few* of my footsteps. He already knows Michael Coe from the chess club; I'd like him to meet Willa Cather from the great plains. He went to camp last summer with Eric Blankenbaker; I'd like him to march through the Deep South with Martin Luther King, Jr. He swaps opinions on a variety of subjects with Marlon Kautz; I'd like him to do the same with Henry Louis Mencken. These are just a few of the people I hope to discuss with him when he's older, in conversations that burst with passion, going on for hours and crying out for resumption the instant they cease. The reader-reader relationship, I am now beginning to see, can be a bond every bit as enduring as the one between reader and writer.

I stand up, walk to the living room window, pull back the drapes. The dogwood has come to life. Hundreds of delicate white flowers, *thousands* of them, have erupted from the tree, each with its four gracefully swooping bracts and its tiny pink fruit. The branches are no longer overwhelmed by the power lines; rather, they have taken on an identity of their own, one that will last for the whole blooming season.

Cailie waves to me. I wave back. She has climbed higher in the tree than I have ever seen her before. She yells, "Can you hear me, Dad?"

I flash a thumbs-up.

"Watch," she says, "I can fly!" and she jumps off her branch like a gutsy little sparrow, landing on the ground with both feet and pitching forward, stopping her momentum with her hands before she tumbles into a somersault. She looks up at me and beams, extending her arms, her lips forming a soft, "Ta-*da!*"

Cailin Burns is six years old on this day in the late spring of 1995, which I suppose means that in a few more years I will give her my childhood edition of *Peter Pan* by Sir James M. Barrie. Assuming, of course, that the tattered old book holds out that long.

I am now certain the story will.

From *The Poetical Works of Henry Wadsworth Longfellow* (Boston: Houghton, Mifflin, 1890), vol. 5, p. 951.

The Joy of Books List

I am not a literary critic, not an academic, not a regular contributor to the *New York Review of Books*. Which is to say that in my reading I am strictly an amateur, but an amateur in the best sense of the word, I like to think—in the sense of being one who, as the *Random House Dictionary of the English Language* puts it, "engages in a study, sport, or other activity for pleasure rather than for financial benefit or professional reasons." That's me, all right: an engager in study for pleasure. There is no financial benefit in my reading; in fact, I bear the the monetary strain of buying so many books. There are no professional reasons for my reading; I seldom pick up a volume that adds to either my material possessions or my public renown. I have no special training as a reader, but much gratitude for the author's gifts and labor; no unique insights, but a galloping enthusiasm.

It is in this spirit—touting my strengths, confessing my weaknesses—that I present a list of 572 books that have given me joy over the years. One gave me joy in the writing, the other 571 in the reading. The number is arbitrary, of course, but then so is the list, which is not meant to replace the Harvard Classics, nor compete with the Great Books curriculum at St. John's College in Maryland. In fact, the list is probably less a public service than a display of self-indulgence.

But perhaps it will inspire some of you to indulge along with me, as if we were a couple of kids trading baseball cards: comparing likes, sharing dislikes, proposing deals to each other. I show you my list, you show me yours. I tell you why I left off Herman Melville yet included Lawrence Sanders; you try to explain omitting John Cheever while finding a place for Peggy Noonan.

A harmless enough diversion, it seems to me, but more than that—stimulating, challenging, a way to keep the faith on a rainy afternoon in a world gone crazy with technology. Just the kind of thing that amateurs like to do.

Fiction

CLASSIC

Anderson, Sherwood	*Winesburg, Ohio*
Aristophanes	*Lysistrata*
Barrie, Sir James M.	*Peter Pan*
Benet, Stephen Vincent	*The Devil and Daniel Webster*
Brontë, Charlotte	*Jane Eyre*
Brontë, Emily	*Wuthering Heights*
Butler, Samuel	*The Way of All Flesh*
Cather, Willa	*Death Comes for the Archbishop*
	A Lost Lady
	My Antonia
	O Pioneers
Crane, Stephen	*The Red Badge of Courage*
Dickens, Charles	*David Copperfield*
	Great Expectations
	Oliver Twist
	A Tale of Two Cities

183

The Joy of Books List

Dostoevsky, Fyodor

The Brothers Karamazov
Crime and Punishment
The Idiot

Doyle, Sir Arthur Conan

The Adventures of
Sherlock Holmes

Dreiser, Theodore

An American Tragedy
Sister Carrie

Dumas, Alexandre

The Three Musketeers

Eliot, George

Middlemarch
Silas Marner

Fielding, Henry

Tom Jones

Fitzgerald, F. Scott

The Great Gatsby
Tender Is the Night

Flaubert, Gustave

Madame Bovary

Hale, Edward Everett

The Man without a Country

Hardy, Thomas

Far from the Madding Crowd
Jude the Obscure
The Mayor of Casterbridge
The Return of the Native
Tess of the D'Urbervilles

Hawthorne, Nathaniel

The House of the Seven Gables
The Scarlet Letter

Hemingway, Ernest

The Sun Also Rises

Hilton, James

Goodbye, Mr. Chips
Lost Horizon

Hugo, Victor	*Les Misérables*
Huxley, Aldous	*Brave New World*
James, Henry	*Daisy Miller*
	The Portrait of a Lady
	Washington Square
Lee, Harper	*To Kill a Mockingbird*
Lewis, Sinclair	*Arrowsmith*
	Babbitt
	Elmer Gantry
	Main Street
	The Man Who Knew Coolidge
Maugham, W. Somerset	*The Moon and Sixpence*
Molière	*The Misanthrope*
Orwell, George	*Animal Farm*
	1984
Poe, Edgar Allan	*Tales of Mystery and Imagination*
Rand, Ayn	*Atlas Shrugged*
	The Fountainhead
Remarque, Erich Maria	*All Quiet on the Western Front*
Scott, Sir Walter	*Ivanhoe*
Shakespeare, William	*Hamlet*
	Macbeth
	The Merchant of Venice
	A Midsummer Night's Dream
	Romeo and Juliet
	The Taming of the Shrew

Shaw, George Bernard	*Back to Methuselah*
	Candida
	Major Barbara
	Man and Superman
	Mrs. Warren's Profession
Steinbeck, John	*Cannery Row*
	East of Eden
	The Grapes of Wrath
	Of Mice and Men
	Tortilla Flat
	The Winter of Our Discontent
Stowe, Harriet Beecher	*Uncle Tom's Cabin*
Swift, Jonathan	*Gulliver's Travels*
Thackeray, William M.	*Vanity Fair*
Tolstoy, Leo	*Anna Karenina*
	War and Peace
Turgenev, Ivan	*Fathers and Sons*
Twain, Mark	*The Adventures of Huckleberry Finn*
	Adventures of Tom Sawyer
	The Prince and the Pauper
Warren, Robert Penn	*All the King's Men*
Waugh, Evelyn	*The Loved One*
	Scoop
Wells, H. G.	*The Invisible Man*

Wharton, Edith	*The Age of Innocence* *Ethan Frome* *The House of Mirth*
Wilder, Thornton	*Our Town*
Wright, Richard	*Native Son*

CONTEMPORARY

Banks, Russell	*The Sweet Hereafter*
Bradbury, Ray	*Dandelion Wine*
Brautigan, Richard	*Dreaming of Babylon* *So the Wind Won't Blow* *It All Away* *Sombrero Fallout* *The Tokyo-Montana Express*
Brown, Rosellen	*Before and After*
Buckley, Christopher	*Thank You for Smoking*
Capote, Truman	*Breakfast at Tiffany's* *In Cold Blood*
Cheever, John	*Oh What a Paradise It Seems* *The Stories of John Cheever*
Dexter, Pete	*The Paperboy* *Paris Trout*

Doctorow, E. L.

Billy Bathgate
Loon Lake
Ragtime
The Waterworks
Welcome to Hard Times

Erdrich, Louise

The Beet Queen

Gates, David

Jernigan

Greene, Graham

The End of the Affair
The Human Factor
The Ministry of Fear
The Quiet American
Travels with My Aunt

Grisham, John

The Chamber

Harrison, Colin

Bodies Electric

Herr, Michael

Walter Winchell

Hijuelos, Oscar

The Mambo Kings
Play Songs of Love

Irving, John

The Cider House Rules
The Hotel New Hampshire
The World According to Garp

Ishiguro, Kazuo

An Artist of the Floating World
The Remains of the Day

Just, Ward

The American Ambassador
Jack Gance

L'Heureux, John

The Shrine at Altamira

Lightman, Alan   *Einstein's Dreams*
                                      Good Benito

Márquez, Gabriel García   *Love in the Time of Cholera*

Martin, David   *The Crying Heart Tattoo*
                                      Tethered

Patrick, Vincent   *Family Business*

Price, Richard   *Clockers*

Salinger, J. D.   *The Catcher in the Rye*

Schulberg, Budd   *What Makes Sammy Run?*

Shapiro, Stanley   *A Time to Remember*

Shaw, Irwin   *Acceptable Losses*
                                      Bread Upon the Waters
                                      Nightwork
                                      Short Stories: Five Decades
                                      The Top of the Hill
                                      Two Weeks in Another Town
                                      Voices of a Summer Day

Stegner, Wallace   *Angle of Repose*

Styron, William   *The Confessions of Nat Turner*
                                      Lie Down in Darkness
                                      Sophie's Choice

Suskind, Patrick   *Perfume*

Taylor, Peter   *A Summons to Memphis*

Theroux, Paul   *The Mosquito Coast*

Turow, Scott — *Presumed Innocent* / *The Burden of Proof*

Tyler, Anne — *The Accidental Tourist* / *Ladder of Years*

Updike, John — *Rabbit at Rest* / *Rabbit Is Rich* / *Rabbit, Run*

Vidal, Gore — *1876* / *Lincoln*

Vonnegut, Kurt — *Breakfast of Champions* / *Cat's Cradle* / *Slaughterhouse Five*

Wolfe, Tom — *The Bonfire of the Vanities*

CONTEMPORARY (GENRE)

Block, Lawrence — *A Dance at the Slaughterhouse* / *The Devil Knows You're Dead* / *Eight Million Ways to Die* / *A Walk among the Tombstones*

Buckley, William F., Jr. — The Blackford Oakes novels

Cook, Thomas H. — *The City When It Rains* / *Evidence of Blood* / *Mortal Memory* / *Night Secrets* / *Streets of Fire*

Crichton, Michael	*Disclosure*
	The Great Train Robbery
	Rising Sun
Gifford, Thomas	*The Assassini*
	The Cavanaugh Quest
	Praetorian
	The Wind Chill Factor
Gifford, Thomas	*Kiss Me Once*
(as Thomas Maxwell)	*Kiss Me Twice*
Goddard, Robert	*Debt of Dishonour*
	Hand in Glove
	Into the Blue
Goldman, William	*Magic*
	Marathon Man
Higgins, George V.	*Cogan's Trade*
	The Friends of Eddie Coyle
	Wonderful Years, Wonderful Years
King, Stephen	*Carrie*
	The Dead Zone
	Different Seasons
	It
	Pet Sematary
	Salem's Lot
	The Shining
Leonard, Elmore	*Bandits*
	Get Shorty
	Glitz
	Stick
	Swag

The Joy of Books List

McBain, Ed	The 87th Precinct novels The Matthew Hope novels
MacDonald, John D.	The Travis McGee novels
Maurier, Daphne du	*Don't Look Now* *The Flight of the Falcon* *The Glassblowers*
Parker, Robert B.	The Spenser novels
Sanders, Lawrence	The Commandment novels The Deadly Sin novels The Archie McNally novels
Stout, David	*Carolina Skeletons* *Night of the Ice Storm*
Stout, Rex	Most of the Nero Wolfe novels
Symons, Julian	*The Blackheath Poisonings* *The Detling Secret* *The Kentish Manor Murders*
Tryon, Thomas	*The Night of the Moonbow* *The Other*
Wambaugh, Joseph	*The Choirboys* *The Delta Star* *Fugitive Nights* *The Glitter Dome* *The Golden Orange* *The Secrets of Harry Bright*

POETRY

Frost, Robert	*Collected Poems of Robert Frost*
Murray, G. E.	*Gasoline Dreams*
	Holding Fast
	Repairs
Stevens, Wallace	*Collected Poems*

Non-Fiction

BIOGRAPHY, AUTOBIOGRAPHY, MEMOIR

Adams, Henry	*The Education of Henry Adams*
Aitken, Jonathan	*Nixon: A Life*
Ambrose, Stephen E.	*Nixon: The Education of a Politician* *Nixon: Ruin and Recovery, 1973–1990* *Nixon: The Triumph of a Politician*
Armstrong, H. C.	*Grey Wolf* (a biography of Ataturk)
Barzini, Luigi	*O America*
Bate, W. Jackson	*Samuel Johnson*
Berg, A. Scott	*Max Perkins: Editor of Genius*
Bower, Catherine Drinker	*The Most Dangerous Man in America* (a biography of Benjamin Franklin)

194

Branden, Barbara	*The Passion of Ayn Rand*
Caro, Robert	*The Power Broker:* *Robert Moses and the* *Fall of New York*
Clark, Ronald W.	*The Life of Bertrand Russell*
Clarke, Gerald	*Capote*
Collier, Peter, and David Horowitz	*The Fords* *The Kennedys* *The Roosevelts:* *An American Saga*
Cowley, Malcolm	*The Dream of the* *Golden Mountains*
Dallek, Robert	*Lone Star Rising:* *Lyndon Johnson* *and His Times, 1908–1960*
Durant, Will and Ariel	*A Dual Autobiography*
Epstein, Daniel Mark	*Sister Aimee*
Esquire magazine, ed.	*Fifty Who Made the Difference*
Fecher, Charles A.	*Mencken: A Study* *of His Thought*
Flexner, James Thomas	*George Washington,* 4 volumes
Frady, Marshall	*Billy Graham*
Franklin, Benjamin	*Autobiography*
Friedrich, Otto	*Glenn Gould: A Life* *and Variations*

The Joy of Books List

Gabler, Neal	*Winchell: Gossip, Power, and the Culture of Celebrity*
Gill, Brendan	*Here at the New Yorker*
Goodwin, Doris Kearns	*The Fitzgeralds and the Kennedys* *Lyndon Johnson and the American Dream*
Hamilton, Nigel	*JFK: Reckless Youth*
Hoff, Joan	*Nixon Reconsidered*
Hoyt, Edwin P.	*The Improper Bostonian* (a biography of Oliver Wendell Holmes)
Humphrey, William	*Farther Off from Heaven* (an autobiography)
Johnson, Paul	*Intellectuals* (biographical essays)
Keats, John	*You Might as Well Live* (a biography of Dorothy Parker)
Lacey, Robert	*Ford: The Men and the Machine*
Lardner, Ring, Jr.	*The Lardners*
Lubow, Arthur	*The Reporter Who Would Be King: Richard Harding Davis*

McCullough, David	*Mornings on Horseback* (a biography of Theodore Roosevelt) *Truman*
Mack, John E.	*A Prince of Our Disorder* (a biography of T. E. Lawrence)
Malone, Dumas	*Jefferson and His Time,* 6 volumes (a biography of Thomas Jefferson)
Manchester, William	*American Caesar* (a biography of Douglas MacArthur) *Disturber of the Peace* (a biography of H. L. Mencken) *The Last Lion,* 2 volumes (a biography of Winston Churchill)
Mellow, James R.	*Invented Lives* (a biography of F. Scott and Zelda Fitzgerald *Nathaniel Hawthorne in His Times*
Mencken, H. L.	*A Choice of Days* (an autobiography)
Milton, Joyce	*Loss of Eden: A Biography of Charles and Anne Morrow Lindbergh*

Morris, Edmund	*The Rise of Theodore Roosevelt*
Oates, Stephen B.	*With Malice toward None* (a biography of Abraham Lincoln)
Parini, Jay	*John Steinbeck*
Reeves, Thomas C.	*The Life and Times of Joe McCarthy* *A Question of Character: A Life of John F. Kennedy*
Smith, Gene	*When the Cheering Stopped: The Last Years of Woodrow Wilson*
Smith, H. Allen	*The Life and Legend of Gene Fowler*
Speer, Albert	*Inside the Third Reich* (an autobiography)
Steinbeck, John	*Travels with Charley* (a memoir)
Swanberg, W. A.	*Citizen Hearst* *Luce and His Empire*
Taylor, Robert Lewis	*Vessel of Wrath* (a biography of Carrie Nation) *W. C. Fields: His Fortunes and Follies*

Teichmann, Howard	*George S. Kaufman* *Smart Aleck* (a biography of Alexander Woollcott)
Thurber, James	*The Years with Ross* (a memoir on Harold Ross)
Tomkins, Calvin	*Eric Hoffer* *Living Well Is the Best Revenge* (a biography of Gerald and Sara Murphy)
Wicker, Tom	*One of Us: Richard Nixon* *and the American Dream*
Wolff, Geoffrey	*Black Sun* (a biography of Harry Crosby) *The Duke of Deception* (a biography of the author's father)
Yagoda, Ben	*Will Rogers*
Yardley, Jonathan	*Ring* (a biography of Ring Lardner)

AMERICAN HISTORY

Allen, Frederick Lewis	*Only Yesterday* *Since Yesterday* *The Big Change*

The Joy of Books List

Amory, Cleveland — *Who Killed Society?*

Behn, Noel — *Lindbergh: The Crime*

Berendt, John — *Midnight in the Garden of Good and Evil*

Beschloss, Michael — *The Crisis Years*
Mayday

Boardman, Barrington — *From Harding to Hiroshima*

Boorstin, Daniel — *The Americans,* 3 volumes

Brooks, John — *The Great Leap*

Coffey, John — *The Long Thirst*

Collier, James Lincoln — *The Rise of Selfishness in America*

Collier, Peter, and David Horowitz — *Destructive Generation*

Commager, Henry Steele — *The American Mind*

Cooper, John Milton, Jr. — *Pivotal Decades: The United States 1900–1920*

Fitzgerald, Frances — *America Revised*

Fried, Richard — *Nightmare in Red*

Furnas, J. C. — *The Americans: 1587–1914*
Great Times
The Life and Times of the Late Demon Rum
Stormy Weather

Gabler, Neal · *An Empire of Their Own: How the Jews Invented Hollywood*

Halberstam, David · *The Best and the Brightest* · *The Powers That Be*

Hart, Jeffrey · *When the Going Was Good!*

Heat Moon, William L. · *Blue Highways*

Isaacson, Walter, and Evan Thomas · *The Wise Men*

Jackson, John A. · *Big Beat: Alan Freed and the Early Years of Rock and Roll*

Kasson, John F. · *Rudeness and Civility: Manners in Nineteenth-Century Urban America*

Kowinski, William Severini · *The Malling of America*

Lerner, Max · *America as a Civilization*

Lipstadt, Deborah · *Beyond Belief*

Lord, Walter · *The Good Years*

McCullough, David · *The Great Bridge* · *The Johnstown Flood* · *The Path between the Seas*

Manchester, William · *The Death of a President* · *The Glory and the Dream*

Miller, Douglas T., and Marion Nowak · *The Fifties*

The Joy of Books List

Mitford, Jessica	*The American Way of Death*
Oakley, Ronald J.	*God's Country:* *America in the Fifties*
Parrish, Michael E.	*Anxious Decades: America in* *Prosperity and Depression,* *1920–1941*
Perrett, Geoffrey	*America in the Twenties*
Radosh, Ronald, and Joyce Milton	*The Rosenberg File*
Rorabaugh, W. J.	*The Alcoholic Republic*
Russell, Francis	*Sacco & Vanzetti*
Schor, Janet B.	*The Overworked American:* *The Unexpected Decline* *of Leisure*
Starr, Kevin	*Americans and the* *California Dream* *Inventing the Dream*
Sullivan, Mark	*Our Times,* 6 volumes
Tocqueville, Alexis de	*Democracy in America,* 2 volumes
Tyndall, George Brown	*America,* 2 volumes
Wolfe, Tom	*The Right Stuff*

WORLD HISTORY

Ackerman, Diane	*The Natural History of the Senses*
Bronowski, Jacob	*The Ascent of Man*
Burns, Michael	*Dreyfus: A Family Affair, 1789–1945*
Darnton, Robert	*The Great Cat Massacre*
Durant, Will and Ariel	*The Lessons of History* *The Story of Civilization,* 11 volumes
Gramont, Sanche de	*The French*
Hadingham, Evan	*Lines to the Mountain Gods: Nazca and the Mysteries of Peru*
Hoving, Thomas	*Tutankhamun: The Untold Story*
Hughes, Robert	*The Fatal Shore*
Johnson, Paul	*The Birth of the Modern* *Modern Times*
Kahn, E. J.	*The China Hands*
Karlen, Arno	*Napoleon's Glands*
Lelyveld, Joseph	*Move Your Shadow*
McPhee, John	*La Place de La Concorde Suisse*
Manchester, William	*The Arms of Krupp* *A World Lit Only by Fire*

The Joy of Books List

Marks, Richard Lee	*Three Men of the Beagle*
Morton, Frederic	*A Nervous Splendor*
	Thunder at Twilight:
	Vienna 1913/1914
Picknett, Lynn, and Clive Prince	*Turin Shroud*
Sachar, Abram L.	*The Course of Our Times*
Sale, Kirkpatrick	*The Conquest of Paradise*
Shipler, David K.	*Russia: Broken Idols,*
	Solemn Dreams
Smith, Hedrick	*The Russians*
Stille, Alexander	*Benevolence and Betrayal:*
	Five Italian Jewish
	Families under Fascism
Tannehill, Reay	*Food in History*
	Sex in History
Tuchman, Barbara	*A Distant Mirror*
	The Guns of August
	The Proud Tower
	Stilwell and the American
	Experience in China
	The Zimmerman Telegram
Weber, Eugen	*France: Fin de Siècle*
Wells, H. G.	*The Outline of History*
Woodham-Smith, Cecil	*The Great Hunger*
	The Reason Why

The Joy of Books List

POLITICS, CURRENT EVENTS, CULTURE, MEDIA

Altschuler, Glenn C., and David I. Grossvogel	*Changing Channels: America in* *TV Guide*
Bennett, William J.	*The Devaluing of America*
Bernstein, Richard	*Dictatorship of Virtue*
Bissinger, H. G.	*Friday Night Lights*
Bloom, Allan	*The Closing of the* *American Mind*
Brownstein, Ronald	*The Power and the Glitter:* *The Hollywood-* *Washington Connection*
Burns, Eric	*Broadcast Blues:* *Dispatches from the* *Twenty-Year War between* *a Television Reporter* *and His Medium*
Carter, Stephen L.	*The Confirmation Mess* *The Culture of Disbelief* *Reflections of an* *Affirmative Action Baby*
Corwin, Norman	*Trivializing America*
Cowley, Malcolm	*The View from Eighty*
D'Souza, Dinesh	*Illiberal Education: The Politics* *of Race and Sex* *on Campus*
Giamatti, A. Bartlett	*Take Time for Paradise*

Henry, William A., III	*In Defense of Elitism*
Hentoff, Nat	*Free Speech for Me— But Not for Thee*
Himmelfarb, Gertrude	*The De-Moralization of Society On Looking into the Abyss*
Hoffer, Eric	*In Our Times The True Believer Truth Imagined*
Howard, Philip K.	*The Death of Common Sense: How Law Is Suffocating America*
Hughes, Robert	*Culture of Complaint*
Jasper, James M., and Dorothy Nelkin	*The Animal Rights Crusade*
Kelly, Brian	*Adventures in Porkland*
Kimball, Roger	*Tenured Radicals*
Kluge, P. F.	*Alma Mater*
Kohn, Alfie	*Punished by Rewards*
Lipstadt, Deborah	*Denying the Holocaust*
Machiavelli, Niccolo	*The Prince*
McKibben, Bill	*The Age of Missing Information*
Mencken, H. L.	*Prejudices,* 6 volumes
O'Rourke, P. J.	*Parliament of Whores*

Paulos, John Allen   *Innumeracy: Mathematical Illiteracy and Its Consequences*

Phillips, Kevin   *Boiling Point*
The Politics of Rich and Poor

Postman, Neil   *Amusing Ourselves to Death: Public Discourse in the Age of Show Business*
Conscientious Objections
Technopoly

Rauch, Jonathan   *Demosclerosis: The Silent Killer of American Government*
Kindly Inquisitors

Roiphe, Katie   *The Morning After*

Ruggerio, Vincent Ryan   *Warning: Nonsense Is Destroying America*

Schickel, Richard   *Intimate Strangers*

Schlesinger, Arthur M., Jr.   *The Disuniting of America*

Smith, Hedrick   *The Power Game*

Sowell, Thomas   *Inside American Education*

Sykes, Charles J.   *A Nation of Victims: The Decay of the American Character*

Tyrrell, R. Emmett , Jr.   *The Liberal Crack-Up*

Wolfe, Tom   *From Bauhaus to Our House*